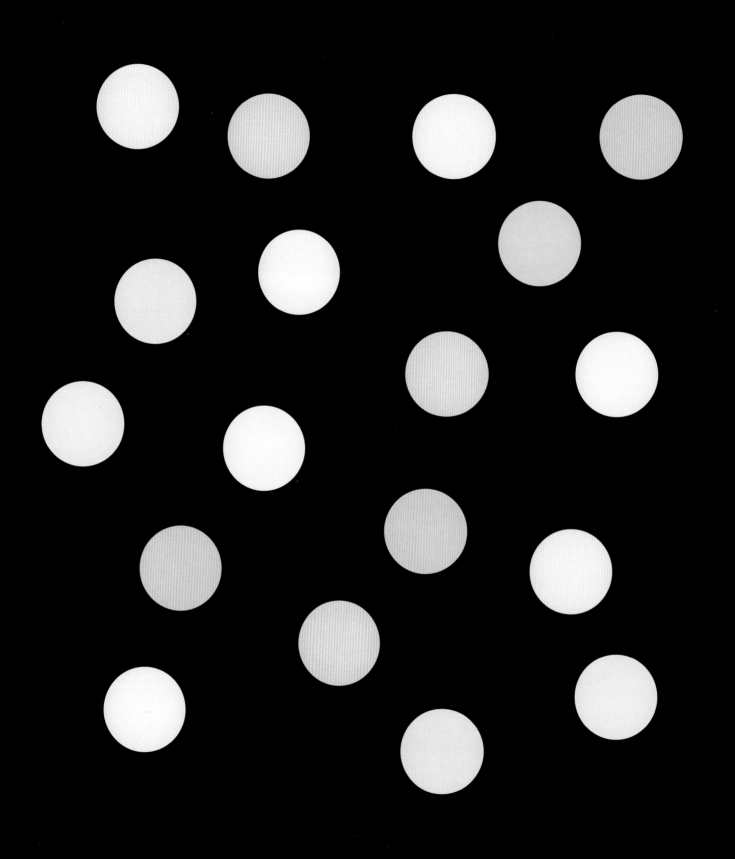

A Brief History of Shorts

The Ultimate Guide to Understanding Your Underwear

JOE BOXER®

CHRONICLE BOOKS

SAN FRANCISCO

Page 92 constitutes a continuation of the copyright page.
Printed in Hong Kong.
Library of Congress Cataloging-in-Publication Data:
Boxer, Joe.
A brief history of shorts : the ultimate guide to understanding your underwear / Joe Boxer.
p.   cm.
ISBN 0-8118-1004-6
1. Underwear—Miscellanea.   2. Underwear—Humor.   I. Title.
GT2073.B69   1995
391'.42—dc20   95-17572
CIP

Book and cover design: Aufuldish & Warinner

Composition: Sara Cambridge

Acknowledgments

Denise Slattery: producer

Cameron Tuttle: writer

Special thanks to the following for their help and contribution to the making of this book:

Genevieve Morgan, researcher; Jim Oda and the Piqua Historical Society;

Bob Blanchard and the National Knitwear Manufacturers' Association; The Fashion Association; Victor De la Rosa;

Phil May; Kirk Jones; Nick Woodman and Nicole Blackmon courtesy of City Agency;

Karen Steffans; and Jock McDonald.

Distributed in Canada by Raincoast Books
8680 Cambie Street
Vancouver, B.C. V6P 6M9

10 9 8 7 6 5 4 3 2 1

Chronicle Books
275 Fifth Street
San Francisco, CA
94103

Dedication

For Margot, Christopher, and India, who make it all worthwhile to change my underwear every day!

JOE BOXER

Contents

It is by no means a **s m a l l** feat that underwear survives as one of the most durable forms of communication in today's modern world. As a pantless hitchhiker on the information highway, with thumb pointed towards the future, underwear stands proud. It is now time, in this most analog of formats, to put the mythology of underwear, as it pertains to American culture, in its place. This book takes a waistband view of history, where we look eye-to-fly with the great underwear visionaries of time. From the perspective of underwear, everything is tabletops and turnstiles, belt loops and belly buttons. Beyond that, there is an entire world where under-wear is a form of intimacy and virility, deep messages and passion, power and strength. This book is an attempt to give underwear its rightful due as the vessel that carries within it the hope of generations to come, and a few other things that we won't discuss.

Nicholas Graham
(aka JOE BOXER)

Chapter One

Underwear Past, Present, and Future

Adam and Eve

*According to the
Underwear Creationists theory,
the Fall of Man
gave rise to underwear.*

The origin and evolution of underwear has been as hotly debated in the halls of academia and the stalls of bathrooms as the origin of humanity itself. Not surprisingly, two legs of thought have emerged as modern historians probe deeper into our underwear, searching the past in an effort to expose the truth.

One leading school of thought, the Underwear Creationists, bases its belief upon the scriptures of the Bible, claiming that underwear first appeared in the Garden of Eden. Their thesis is simple: In the beginning, there was an end—and it needed to be covered. Soon there were two ends. And so on. Creation theorists argue that the many thousands of paintings of Adam and Eve wearing leafy branches over their loins reflect our enduring fascination not with the Fall of Man, but rather with the rise of underwear.

Underwear Evolutionists dispute the creation theory, believing instead that underwear evolved, cell by cell, over millions of years from a primitive organism, much like humanity. Over time, they posit, Homo sapiens and underwear developed along parallel lines, intersecting every few million years. Some Evolutionists attribute the development of the opposing digit to the need to pull up the early, looser forms of underwear. While underwear archaeologists have unearthed many remnants of ancient briefs, some dating back nearly two million years, there is still a missing link in underwear's evolution.

There is evidence, in fact, to support both of these theories, though neither can be proved beyond doubt. This book does not attempt to resolve the eternal underwear debate but rather to present all of the available information. An individual's underwear beliefs are a personal matter and should be carefully considered. Only after reading the facts in the pages ahead can you decide which underwear theory is closest to the truth.

Despite the opposing theories on underwear's origins, one thing is certain: Wherever people appeared, underwear soon followed.

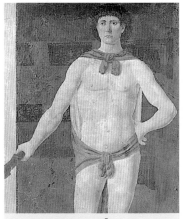

Hercules

Della Francesca's classical painting of Hercules suggests that the mythological character drew his incredible, "superhero" strength from his underwear, which doubled as a cape.

As humans began walking upright, exposing their privates for the first time, they found a need to protect them from the elements and predators. For men, this need led to the first form of underwear, best described as an apron. The apron, which protected against campfire accidents, consisted of a flap of hide, fur, or for very lucky guys, a snake skin hanging from a tether around the waist.

During this period, women's underwear was identical to that worn by men. Through the years, however, the fickle demands of women's fashions gave rise to a multitude of feminine undergarments too vast to be addressed in this volume.

Primitive forms of men's underwear were worn more for decoration than for warmth or protection, reflecting man's earliest desire to escape uniformity and his need to conceal his sense of inferiority. In addition to fur and hide, seashells were a common genital ornament, popular because they never needed laundering and carried with them the sound of the ocean.

Later came the loincloth, which could be wrapped between the legs and secured around the waist, providing more support than an apron. The loincloth not only looked smart but also enabled men to run faster, jump higher, and better elude their predators. Charles Darwin was the first to link underwear to evolution, citing it as an example "survival of the fittest." According to Darwin's theory, individuals with better-fitting underwear survived, producing offspring, while others with poor-fitting underwear died out.

Sumo Wrestlers

The origin of sumo wrestling has been traced back to primitive life when male superiority within a tribe was determined during competitions in which each man tried to strip the others of their underwear.

The History of Underwear Timeline

1500 B.C. Egyptians wear plain linen loincloths, wrapped in the front from right to left. Immaculate underwear is of utmost importance since body cleanliness is a religious ideal among the Egyptians.

A.D. 1100 The first documentation of underwear, made of linen, hemp or silk, appears.

1554 Medieval knights joust in chain mail underwear.

1633 Saxons wear drawers, or "braies," with drawstring waists. ➤

Zulu Headman

Primitive forms of underwear served a decorative function, reflecting man's desire to flout conformity and to conceal his sense of inadequacy.

After a lot of surviving and offspring producing, the loincloth was replaced by the short tunic, or chiton. Early Egyptian, Greek, and Roman underwear was an integral part of that era's fashion and was designed to show from beneath a man's toga. The tunic, much like a short skirt, allowed for easy flashing, which many Romans did as a casual greeting. This popular practice was actually misquoted in William Shakespeare's play, *Julius Caesar;* Mark Antony is recorded elsewhere addressing the crowd at Caesar's funeral, "Friends, Romans, countrymen, show me your rears...." Not until hundreds of years later would revealing one's underwear become a source of shame and embarrassment.

Through the ages, concern for personal hygiene has ebbed and flowed, and so, consequently, has interest in wearing underwear. The Renaissance, a period of rapid cultural development, saw a revival in art, architecture, and underwear. The Saxons wore drawers, or braies, to fend off the chill in cold English castles. While jousting or in battle, medieval knights protected the family jewels with chain mail beneath their armor.

It wasn't until the 17th century that cleanliness became desirable, and people began wearing a light, easily laundered undergarment beneath their outer layers of clothing. Initially, these undergarments were worn to protect the outer layer of clothing from the body's moisture rather than the body from coarse clothing. Initially, most underwear was made of wool. But wool was soon replaced by silk or linen because they were less likely to harbor lice.

Early in the 19th century, enlightened men and women considered underwear to be a sign of status. Owning many pairs distinguished the members of one class from another, and only royalty and members of the upper class owned more than a few undergarments. This lasted until the American Revolution, when standards of personal hygiene improved. At this time, underwear usually was washed weekly, whether it needed it or not.

Sistine Chapel

During the controversial cleaning and restoration of the ceiling of the Sistine Chapel in the 1980s, a zealous workman named Gipeto Olivieri uncovered a startling finding. In Michelangelo's original rendering of The Creation of Adam, *God was actually handing Adam a divine pair of underwear. Shortly after Olivieri's discovery, he fell to his death in a tragic scaffolding accident. The Vatican has denied all rumors surrounding the underwear discovery.*

Former President George Bush

While president of the United States, George Bush and first lady Barbara often secretly tested experimental underwear designs for the military. "Five days!" exclaimed George and Barbara Bush, when asked how long they'd been wearing the army's new self-cleaning underwear.

1893 B.V.D. introduces the first union suit, eliminating annoying underwear slippage.
1908 Drawstring undershorts cut just above the knee become the rage.

1910 Jockey introduces union suits with the "Kenosha Klosed Krotch," two pieces of fabric overlapping in an X.

1914 Boxer shorts with buttons are issued to infantrymen for summer wear in World War I. They're so comfortable, men refuse to wear anything else upon return to the U.S. ➥

Nicolaus Copernicus (1473–1543), the Polish astronomer who first demonstrated that the earth revolves around the sun, often diagrammed the stars in the night sky. On a cold evening in 1522 after a prolonged period of sleep deprivation, Copernicus saw the constellations in the shapes of underwear and charted them as such in his diary. He later discarded his notes on underwear constellations, considering them shortsighted. But his young apprentice, Romulous, sensed their importance and rescued the papers from the fire. Copernicus' original map of the underwear constellations is stored in a vault at the Smithsonian in Washington, D.C.

On a clear night, you can see the underwear constellations that Copernicus first noted in 1522.

Phases of the Moon

| New Moon | Wedging Crescent | 1st Quarter | Wedging Gibbous | Full Moon |

Amazing Underwear Trivia (All True)

1. What Gangster wore bullet-proof shorts?

2. What did soldiers in WW II often display on their underwear?

3. What surplus material was used during WW II by civilians at home to patch holes in underwear?

4. According to the Utility Plan established during WW II, how many coupons were required to "buy" a pair of underwear?

5. How much does the average brief shrink in the dryer?

6. What is the life expectancy of a typical pair of men's underwear?

7. According to a recent national survey, what percentage of men's underwear sales come from briefs? What percentage come from boxers?

8. What is the most popular color of men's underwear?

9. What common liquid, which contains ammonia, was used to clean and bleach underwear in the 17th century?

10. In Painesville, Ohio, a man was convicted of stealing men's underwear. How many pairs did he steal?

Answers

1. Al Capone
2. their national flag
3. parachutes
4. 4
5. 6 to 8%
6. 2 to 3 years
7. briefs, 75 %; boxers, 15%
8. white
9. stale urine
10. over 400 pairs

(In at least one case, he cut the briefs off a sleeping man.)

The full impact of underwear on modern society, which has been obscured over the years, is quite staggering. Underwear was, in fact, the spark that ignited the Industrial Revolution early in the 19th century. Even though no one was talking about underwear, everyone started wearing it.

As the demand for clean, durable underwear surged, cottage industries could no longer fulfill America's appetite. Factories were built, greatly increasing production, and the workforce expanded to include women and children. By the middle of the century, electric-powered knitting machines had been developed to make more underwear even faster.

Underwear was popular but it wasn't perfect. It shifted up, it scooched down, it rolled from side to side and bunched up into uncomfortable wads. Drawers, the predominant style of the day, consisted of two tubes of fabric, open at the crotch and held up by a draw-string waist. The opening was convenient but drafty. Something had to be done.

In 1893, the union suit, the first all-in-one underwear, was invented, putting an end to annoying underwear "slippage." The union suit was ideal for cold weather but too hot for warm climates and rather difficult to get in and out of. Consequently, short underwear separates continued to be updated as an alternative to the union suit. After the turn of the century, as men began to wear short pants for athletic endeavors, button-fly breeches with a closed crotch took off.

By this time, hand laundry could not keep pace with the flow of soiled shorts. Industrial laundries were constructed, further advancing American industry. Naturally, more wash cycles required more soap, which spawned another industry, packaged goods.

Like many important products, underwear was significantly improved by war. In World War I, the first boxer shorts with buttons were issued to infantrymen for summer wear. They were so popular that men insisted on wearing them when they returned home. It wasn't until the mid 1930s that the first brief appeared on the underwear scene. Inspired by swimsuits worn on the French Riviera,

1914 Sigmund Freud publishes his theory on "boxer envy," a psychological disorder suffered by some women who repress their secret desire to wear men's undershirts.

1920 Athletic-style shorts come into vogue, giving birth to the first knee-length drawers with buttons.

1930 "Singletons," a shorter version of the union suit, are introduced. ➤

briefs were cut short and fit snugly. At the time, they were considered nothing more than a short-lived fad by industry observers. But the common man proved the experts wrong, and briefs sold like hotcakes.

World War II also left its mark on underwear. During the war, the first colored boxer shorts (now with elastic waistbands) were issued. Although they were available only in olive drab, they introduced the concept of color to men's underwear. Printed, whimsical patterns soon followed. By the 1950s, men began to enjoy humorous underwear, giving birth to the expression, "It's an inside joke."

Our insatiable appetite for new and better underwear styles propelled chemical companies to develop synthetic fibers, leading to popular nylon and mesh underwear in the 1960s. Since then, designers have subtly improved upon briefs and boxer shorts, even mating the best of both styles in the hybrid boxer-brief.

Although today's man has a veritable smorgasbord of underwear options to choose from, his ever-expanding lifestyle needs are sure to spawn new designs down the road. Even if some designs are unsuccessful, they are all a symbol of humanity's progress.

Tireless human ingenuity combined with advancements in other industries spawned a wave of short-lived underwear designs in the latter half of the twentieth century.

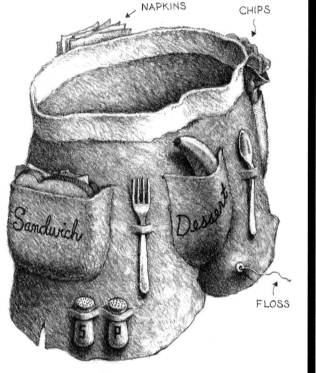

NAPKINS

CHIPS

Sandwich

Dessert

FLOSS

Rotatable Three-legged Shorts

By rotating each leg, shorts could be worn for months without laundering.

Scratch and Sniff Shorts

Designed to conceal odors with just a scratch, but only professional athletes felt free to scratch in public.

Lunch Box-er Shorts

Side pockets for a sandwich, fruit, and chips were convenient, but body heat often warmed mayonnaise, causing hundreds of cases of botulism.

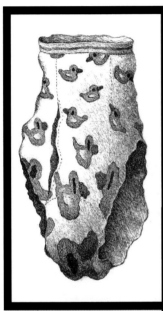

Silly-Putty Shorts

*One pair could be reshaped
into different styles
and patterns, but it tended to
droop dangerously
low in minutes.*

⊔

**Velcro
Fly
Closure**

Ouch!

⊔

Chia-Pet
Underwear

*Just seed, water, and watch
them grow. Unfortunately, fore-
play in these briefs was a lot
like pulling weeds.*

⊔

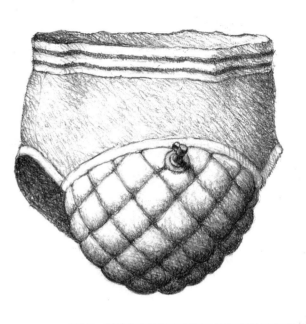

Stadium Shorts

*The padded seat was comfortable but
tended to inspire jeers, such as
"Hey, bubble butt!"*

⊔

The Boxer Sock

*Shorts with a sock attached seemed
like a sensible design. The sock, however, often
mysteriously disappeared in
the laundry.*

⊔

Throughout

the ages, underwear styles have had a tremendous influence on attitudes and behavior, giving rise to new trends and new ideas. But until now, few people have acknowledged underwear's role in society and pop culture. A quick look at the past five decades shows just how much underwear has influenced the men who wear it.

The '50s ☛

Popular underwear styles were tight and white, and so were the predominant values of the decade. Underwear's uniformity contributed to mass conformity, traditional, conservative behavior, and pained expressions on the faces of many.

The '60s

Radical, new underwear styles, such as the thong and the bikini brief, caused radical behavior among a new generation of young men determined to challenge the system. More comfortable underwear led to sit-ins, where thousands of people gathered to share their thoughts on underwear, drop their pants, and drop acid.

The '70s

Advertisements emphasizing underwear's sexuality ignited a sexual revolution. As never before, men were worshiped as sex symbols and often expressed their newfound sexuality in wildly popular nightclubs known as "discos."

The '80s

Underwear prices rose significantly and waistbands expanded, stimulating the national economy and inflating stock and property values across the country. Since so many people were so excited about making money that they often had to go to the bathroom, the decade was labeled "the Go-Go '80s."

The '90s

Men's underwear comes into its own and comes out, inspiring everyone to flaunt their shorts. Pop stars brazenly perform in their undies. Teenagers opt for baggy pants worn at the hip to show off their grundies. Even professional athletes, notoriously shy about underwear, proudly compete in stylish longer briefs.

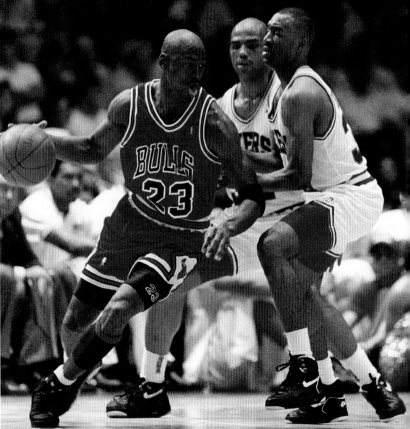

Sociologists are predicting a growing interest in and a wider acceptance of underwear as we approach the next millennium, leading to an increased demand for fresh underwear. This, in turn, will dramatically change the way underwear is designed, manufactured, and distributed in the global marketplace.

Plans are already in the works to install underwear dispensing machines in airport terminals, hotel lobbies, gas stations, and commuter trains in order to accommodate travelers on the go. And don't be surprised to see fast-food chains, movie-theater snack bars, and ballpark concession stands selling underwear in an effort to capitalize on our impulsive cravings.

Underwear is also expected to influence local and national politics. As politicians react to public underwear pressure and the persuasive power of lobbying groups, such as the National Underwear

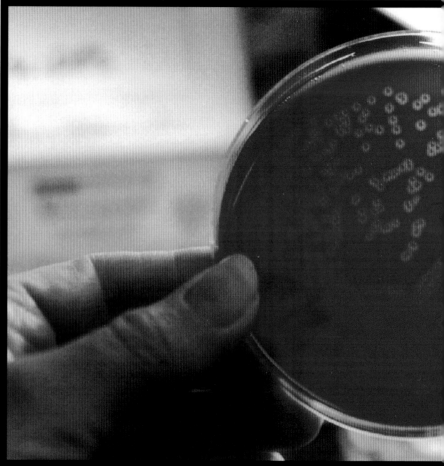

Association (NUA), they will be forced to declare their views on underwear. Some candidates may run on either a boxer or brief platform in an effort to build voter support.

World diplomacy will feel the snugging effects of underwear unification, causing world leaders to align themselves with popular styles. The United States, England, Germany, and Japan are reportedly discussing the possibility

of naming underwear ambassadors, positions that no doubt would be eagerly sought by elder statesmen. If international underwear diplomacy takes hold, the United Nations (UN) is expected to change its name to the United Underwear Nations (UUN).

Underwear appreciation is bound to improve day-to-day life for the average citizen as well. Underwear futures will be traded on the commodities exchange. Banks will give car and home-improvement loans and extend lines of credit based on a person's clean underwear history. Commuters will ride safely and comfortably to work in their underwear, slipping into business attire at the office. In the evenings and on weekends, people will feel free to entertain, garden, exercise, and shop in their underwear.

With time, underwear may even overcome prejudice as people realize that, regardless of race, nationality, or religious beliefs, we all wear underwear. Experts agree that the future of underwear on a personal, national, and global level depends upon change. When it comes to underwear, gradual change is good, but daily change is even better.

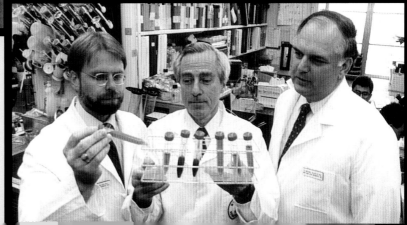

In the years ahead, underwear development will be limited only by the Peter Principle and our imagination. Through the rapidly advancing technology of virtual underwear reality, designers today are able to look ahead and see the future of our behinds simply by donning goggles and a glove. With the flick of a switch, suddenly the end is at hand and the underwear frontier splits wide open, revealing a bottomless pit of design possibilities.

Experts Predict...

Cellular shorts: *make and receive phone calls in your shorts.*

No-more-beeper briefs: *silently vibrates when you get an important call.*

Fat-free underwear: *measures your percentage of body fat every hour.*

(If your fat percentage rises, your shorts constrict.)

Self-cleaning shorts: *contain time-released, bacteria-killing scent buds.*

Organic Underwear: *must lie fallow every third season.*

Free-range underwear: *farmed and fed naturally, fresh but a little tough.*

Two-step underwear: *counts out the steps for you.*

Twelve-step underwear: *abstains from abusive behavior so you don't have to.*

Cruelty-free underwear: *never pinches, bunches, or binds.*

Crystal clear underwear: *no one knows if it's better, but marketing loves it.*

Gravity-free underwear: *keeps you in stitches inside your britches.*

Interactive underwear: *strikes up conversations with attractive women for you.*

Short-stack shorts: *body heat warms the pancake breakfast built right in. Perfect for the guy on the go.*

Liquid underwear: *changes form depending upon the temperature.*

Telecommuting underwear: *travels to and from the office while you stay home.*

Virtual underwear: *you think you're wearing underwear but you're not.*

Saves on laundry and has no visible panty lines.

The Wonderbrief: *structurally designed pouch enhances the size of a man's package.*

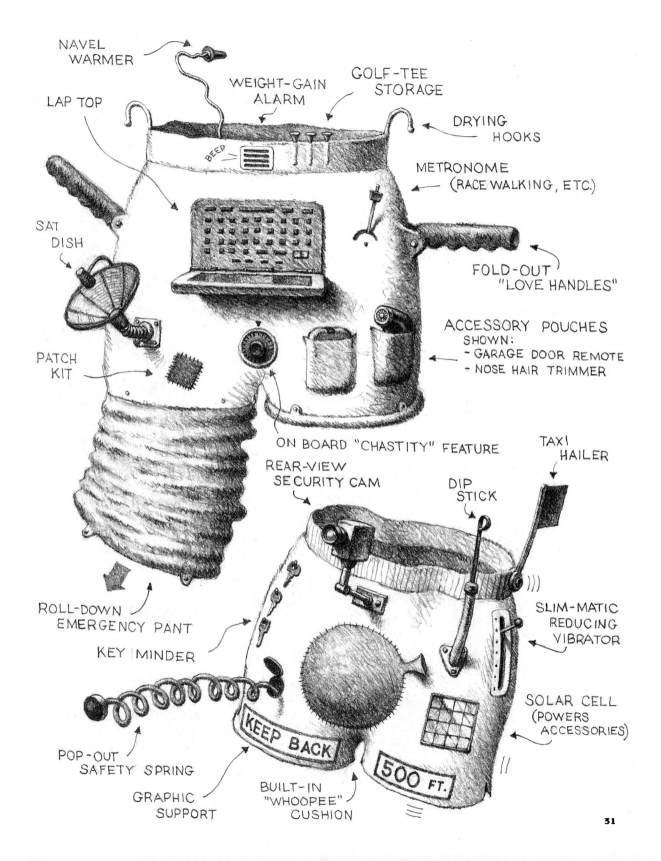

NAVEL WARMER

WEIGHT-GAIN ALARM

GOLF-TEE STORAGE

LAP TOP

DRYING HOOKS

BEEP

METRONOME (RACE WALKING, ETC.)

SAT DISH

FOLD-OUT "LOVE HANDLES"

PATCH KIT

ACCESSORY POUCHES
SHOWN:
- GARAGE DOOR REMOTE
- NOSE HAIR TRIMMER

ON BOARD "CHASTITY" FEATURE

TAXI HAILER

REAR-VIEW SECURITY CAM

DIP STICK

ROLL-DOWN EMERGENCY PANT

SLIM-MATIC REDUCING VIBRATOR

KEY MINDER

SOLAR CELL (POWERS ACCESSORIES)

KEEP BACK

POP-OUT SAFETY SPRING

500 FT.

GRAPHIC SUPPORT

BUILT-IN "WHOOPEE" CUSHION

When Sigmund Freud published

When Sigmund Freud published his theory on "boxer envy" in 1913, women were outraged. At that time, no woman would admit her repressed secret desire to wear men's underwear. But further research on the subject indicates that many women do wear men's undershorts, and some have accomplished great things in them. Access to personal diaries and interviews with close friends have produced the following list of famous and infamous women believed to have worn boxers.

Match the women with their short encounters:

Eva Peron	Wrote *The Autobiography of Ernest Hemingway's Shorts*
Leona Helmsley	Frequently addressed the United Nations General Assembly wearing plaid shorts
Madonna	Believed her shorts were divinely inspired
Eleanor Roosevelt	Often exclaimed, "Holy Shorts, Batman!"
Joan of Arc	Forgot to wear her lucky shorts on an ill-fated flight over the Pacific
Gertrude Stein	Favored shorts with flowers and cow-skull prints
Amelia Earhart	Ruled her New York "Palace" with iron shorts
Bat Girl	Concealed her secret shorts from Argentina and Broadway
Georgia O'Keeffe	Performs on and off stage in men's shorts

1931 Secret societies of gentlemen underwear golfers, often gathering in back lots, become popular during prohibition

Underwear Sequels

As Americans develop new, more meaningful relationships with their underwear, they will want to see these relationships portrayed on the screen and in literature. In anticipation of the public demand for underwear information and entertainment, many writers, filmmakers, and artists are already hard at work, developing underwear sequels. Here are the names of just a few:

- My Own Private Underwear
- Pair 54, Where Are You?
- War and Briefs
- The Britches of Madison County
- A Current Underwear Affair
- I Was a Teenage Underwear Wolf
- The Pelican Boxer Brief

- Real Men Don't Eat Underwear
- Saturday Short Fever
- Beauty and the Brief
- Underwear Styles of the Rich and Famous
- To Catch a Brief
- The Short Also Rises
- The Brady Bunched Brief
- Home Underwear Improvement

1932 The charismatic midget ☞ and underwear manufacturer Robert "Shorty" Calhoun is arrested after his Shorts By Shorties underwear company is implicated in numerous violations of child labor laws.

1935 Inspired by swimsuits worn on the French Riviera, Jockey develops and patents the inverted Y-front brief, labeled a fad by the competition. Marshall & Field Co. sells 30,000 pairs of briefs in three months.

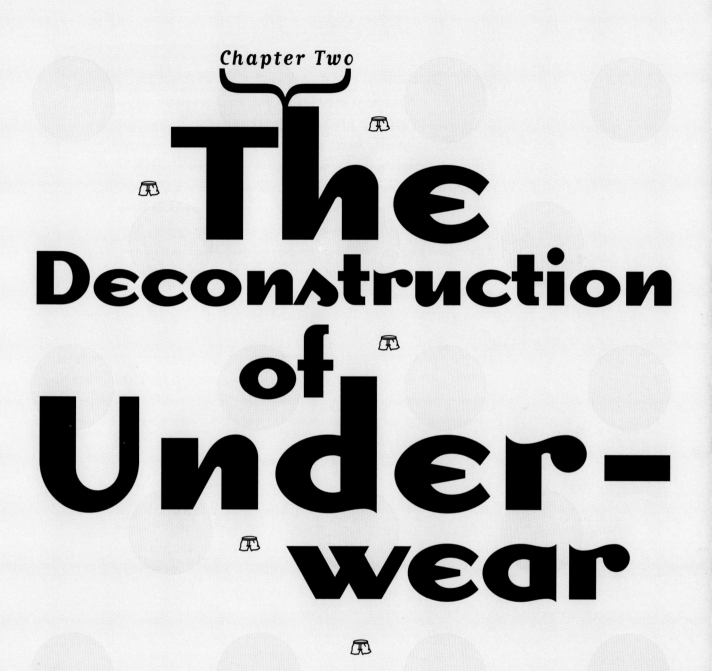

Chapter Two

The Deconstruction of Under-wear

There are a thousand different stories in the underwear city. Every pair—no matter how large or small, how plain or plaid, how cheap or over-priced—is a unique creation with a unique history and point of view. Every pair has roots reaching hundreds of miles and a few months, maybe even a year, into the past. Yet few people ever stop to consider their underwear's incredible journey from the cotton field to their home. Why? Because of fear.

Most men are afraid of real intimacy, afraid of getting too close and being hurt, afraid of knowing too much about the very piece of clothing that protects them from scratchy fabrics, absorbs dangerous body moisture, and cradles their very manhood. But you don't have to be like most men. Look fear straight in the fly and see beyond the elastic waistband, the ribbed trim, and the 100% knit cotton panels. Drop your pants and build a bond with your boxers or briefs that a million washes and tumbles in a hot dryer can't destroy.

Sure, you could have a casual relationship, going from one pair to the next, knowing little more than color and size. Or you could choose a more rewarding path by making a commitment and exploring your underwear's rich and poignant past.

Ponder the sadness your underwear must have felt as just a little cotton ball plucked from the field. Try to imagine the loneliness and pain of the underwear factory—woven by cold machinery, pierced by sharp needles, and thrown into bins with lots of strange underwear. Unless you take the time to explore your underwear's roots, you'll never understand the insecurity it felt sitting on a shelf, waiting to be chosen, or the joy it felt when you took it home in your arms.

All it takes is desire and a little time. Go to the store where you first met and fondly look around. Visit the factory where it was made and talk with the woman who first folded your underwear. Travel to the cotton field and find the man who harvested the little cotton balls. If you commit yourself to your underwear, it will know how much you care and be behind you all the way.

A Day in the Life of a Pair of Underwear

Each underwear experience is unique. This is just one pair's story:

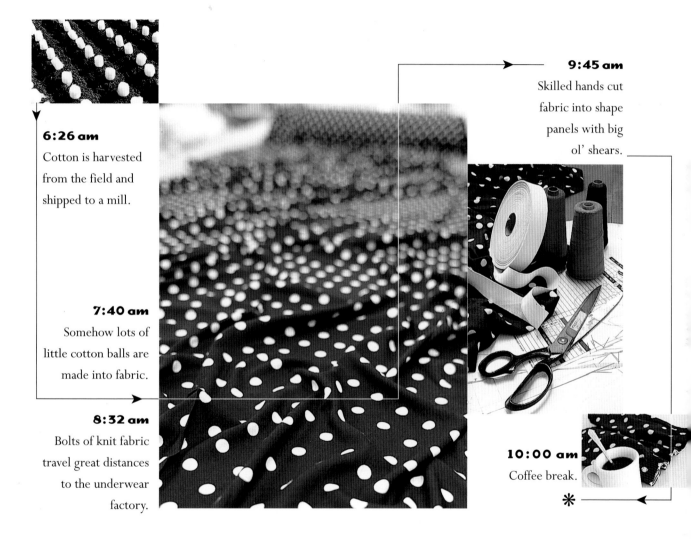

9:45 am
Skilled hands cut fabric into shape panels with big ol' shears.

6:26 am
Cotton is harvested from the field and shipped to a mill.

7:40 am
Somehow lots of little cotton balls are made into fabric.

8:32 am
Bolts of knit fabric travel great distances to the underwear factory.

10:00 am
Coffee break.

1937 The coronation of George VI sets off a short-lived rage of red, white, and blue underwear in Britain.

1939 World War II brings the first colored boxer shorts. Unfortunately, the color is olive drab.

1941 Underwear rationing begins in order to conserve elastic for the war. Knit "utility underwear" proves to be pretty darn comfortable. ➤

11:33 am
Elastic waistbands
are welded (or some-
thing like that) to
underwear.

10:15 am
Really fast needles
with miles of
thread stitch
panels together.

12:00 pm
Underwear rides
zippy conveyor belt
to cafeteria for
lunch.

1:00 pm
Underwear is
inspected by a
really nice lady
named Bertha.

2:05 pm
Bertha's friend
Bernice neatly folds
and stuffs them into
a package.

*

1944 Fighter pilots of the Third Airborne
Division, renowned for flying in only their
underwear, celebrate after completing their
34th mission over France.

1945 Women working in American underwear
factories send notes with underwear shipments to
U.S. soldiers fighting the trenches in France.
Many receive marriage proposals in response. ➤➤

3:00 pm
Underwear rides in a
big, noisy truck
to the store.

4:20 pm
Zoned-out stock boy
transports underwear
to the shelf.

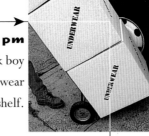

5:55 pm
You see under-
wear, fall madly in
love, and carry
them to a cashier.

7:00 pm
You take them
home in a cool car
you're still making
payments on.

6:30 pm
Sales person with
major attitude rings
up underwear.

11:38 pm
You go home alone, make your underwear a peanut butter and
jelly sandwich, and go to bed.

8:18 pm
You and your underwear head
out looking for action.

9:39 pm
You eat, drink, and boogy. Your
underwear gets hot and soggy.

10:41 pm
You and
your underwear
party on but
meet no one.

The styles of underwear available today are as varied as the men who wear them. Whether you're tight and white, long and strong, or wobble to and fro, there's sure to be a style that's right for you.

Briefs

This classic is scientifically designed to provide correct masculine support without cramping or pinching. Many models come with an inverted-Y fly.

Prince Albert in a Can

You'll feel like royalty when you sport this 100% recyclable model. But watch out for metal detectors! With a friend, you can play telephone, too.

Hose Mitten

Innovated by an entrepreneurial bachelor who finally found a use for those socks widowed in the laundry and for newspaper rubber bands.

Boxer-Briefs

This hybrid style (and relatively new addition to the universe) is a lot like a brief with longer legs so you can't get your undies in a bundle.

Boxer Shorts

Inspired by trunks worn by professional boxers, these shorts afford a greater range of movement for the hang-loose kind of guy.

The Thong

This minimalist model provides maximum ventilation without the risk of those unsightly panty lines.

Colossal Dog

Hold the sauerkraut! This ballpark favorite is guaranteed to keep you warm and toasty long after the seventh-inning stretch.

Bikini Briefs

Known as the Italian stallion of underwear, it keeps you front and center without restricting circulation.

Catcher in the Raw

Designed for hard-core jocks, with a padded pouch that provides excellent protection against curve balls, counter tops, and turnstiles.

Lunch Bunch

Only Faye Wray could resist you in this incredible, edible underwear, an organic alternative to basic cotton briefs.

1946 The term "bikini" first comes into use as bikini-style briefs are designed for men and women.

1952 A strange courting ritual, known as "brief dating," emerges on college campuses across the Midwest, causing hopeful young men to remove their underwear and proudly display them to young women driving past. Dates are chosen based upon the whiteness of their underwear. ➤➤

With landfills

With landfills reaching maximum capacity, it's everyone's civic duty to recycle their underwear. Fortunately, underwear recycling is gaining favor in corporate America, and the technology is advancing rapidly. In the next few years, don't be surprised to see remnants of your old favorites showing up in composite park benches, recycled paper, and shopping bags. But until then, there are plenty of ways that you can recycle your underwear at home.

Just because your briefs have lost their shape and snap doesn't make them useless. Your old underwear deserve a better future than washing and waxing the car. So don't just retire your underwear to the rag bin—recycle with dignity.

Helen mixed diced underwear in with her garden mulch. Marge didn't.

Printed underwear applied to interior walls create an elegant effect.

Professional roofers use old underwear to patch tough holes.

Ten Ways to Recycle Your Underwear

❶ Shred and fluff to make a cozy bed for a pet.

❷ Laminate and use as a mouse pad for your personal computer.

❸ Dice and add to garden mulch.

❹ Cover with paste and apply to walls instead of wallpaper.

❺ Stitch pairs together and make a shower curtain, throw rug, sofa slip cover, or patio umbrella.

❻ Fill with soil and plant with flowers.

❼ Repair holes in your roof.

❽ Knot together and make a hammock.

❾ With two bungee cords, make into a baby swing.

❿ Mail out twenty pairs to friends for good luck instead of a chain letter.

Underwear Abducted by Aliens

Last Friday, I was driving home from Doggy Dee-Lite, where I work the 7 pm. to 2 am. shift. It was around 3 am. when I saw this white glow in the sky about a hundred yards ahead of me, hovering over a field. The glow got brighter and brighter like it was calling out to me. I got out of my truck and stood there for a second--I knew right then and there, something strange was going on. My underwear was shaking like a beagle in heat. The white glow was about 10 feet above the ground when these two glow blobs dropped out. They hit the ground like eggs, cracking open, and a pink stinky vapor rose up out of each one. The vapor floated up, and two aliens were standing there. One of them said, "Free to be, you and me. Free to be, you and me." That's all I remember.

Just before dawn, I woke up lying in the soft dirt next to my truck. My pants were on, but I realized that my underwear was gone. Is that freaky or what?

Sincerely,
John P.

PS. I do not take drugs or alcohol.

My Near-Death Underwear Experience

While helicopter skiing in the Bugaboos, I was buried alive in the snow. I frantically tried to dig myself out but had no idea which way was up. Then, I remembered I had an extra pair of underwear in the pocket of my parka. I was able to push back and eat enough snow to create a tiny pocket of air. I managed to reach the underwear, which I wadded up and then released to see which direction they would fall. Gravity pulled them to the left, I dug to the right and was able to free myself from what was very nearly an icy grave. Without a doubt, that underwear saved my life.

Sincerely,
Wade J.

How My Underwear Hooked a Big One

Last summer I was fishing in Red Rock Reservoir. I hadn't had a strike all day so I floated out to deep waters in an inner tube, hoping to see some action. After a half hour or so I still hadn't had any luck when I felt something brush against my leg and then into my cut-offs. I reached down with one hand and clamped down the end of my shorts and trapped what I hoped was a fish. I couldn't figure out how to get in into my net without dropping my pole, so I wrangled it into my briefs where it stayed until I paddled back to shallow water. When I got to shore, I pulled a 14-inch speckled trout out of my underwear—the same pair I'd been wearing all week.

Wayne B.
Piggit, Arkansas

Proud Parents of Twins

For fourteen years, my husband and I had been trying to have a child, without any success. We had seen every fertility specialist in the state and undergone every possible test, but nothing seemed to help. One day, my husband went to the podiatrist to get a bunion removed and happened to mention our sad plight. The doctor asked if he wore briefs or boxer shorts, then explained that briefs are too warm and cozy for some fellas, and that it can make their sperm count low.

Howard switched to boxer shorts. What the heck—we had nothing to lose. I got pregnant the next month with twins! Howard was so thrilled he handed out boxer shorts to our friends instead of cigars.

Very Truly Yours,
Melanie J.

The Underwear Index

Number of underwear landfills in America:

17

Percentage of people who have a lucky
pair of underwear:

67

Ratio of those who wear boxer shorts to those
who wear briefs:

1:4

Percentage of Americans who would designate their tax
dollars to reduce the National Underwear Debt:

35

Percentage of people who have participated
in a panty raid:

44

Number of Americans who donated their used
underwear to charity in 1993:

1

Percentage of people whose life has been improved
by underwear:

93

Average number of pairs owned by an American
male in a lifetime:

804

Average number of pairs owned by a third-world
male in a lifetime:

212

Percentage of men who have worn women's
underwear at least once:

73

Percentage of women who have worn men's
underwear at least once:

14

Number of pairs of briefs needed to build a stack as tall
as the Empire State Building:

192,854

Percentage of people who wear hand-me-down
underwear:

27

Ratio of people who wear patterned shorts to
those who wear plain white shorts:

6:1

Number of people who claim to have seen Elvis's
underwear since his death:

9

Percentage of men who wear the same pair
for more than one day:

34

Percentage of women who wear the same pair
for more than one day:

2

Number of pairs of underwear knotted together
to make a hammock:

64

Percentage of people who think all nude statues should
be covered with underwear:

19

Percentage of people who would pay more for
cruelty-free underwear:

32

Percentage of people who would buy
disposable underwear:

58

Percentage of people who want to be reincarnated
as a pair of underwear:

6

Percentage of people who believe they were a pair
underwear in a past life:

9

The state where underwear is most likely to be
used to commit murder:

Missouri

Percentage of people who buy underwear from catalogs:

24

Most pairs of briefs worn at one time:

227

Percentage of people who have stolen a lover's
pair of underwear:

63

Estimated number of pairs of size-36 briefs
needed to fill the Grand Canyon:

97,884,367,189

Ratio of boxers to briefs worn in the Senate:

1:9

Ratio of boxers to briefs worn in the
House of Representatives:

1:3

Number of Americans who have lost their
underwear at the movies:

318

Number of pairs of underwear manufactured
in the U.S. each hour:

347

Chances that a person admitted to a U.S. emergency
room is not wearing underwear:

1 in 4

Number of countries in which the average life
expectancy of a pair of underwear is less
than six months:

37

Amount paid for a pair of silk boxer shorts owned by
Andy Warhol at a Sotheby's auction in 1989:

$14,500

Chances that a rock musician performing on-stage is not
wearing underwear:

1 in 3

Chapter Three

Under- wear Make- overs

Does underwear make the man or woman? See for yourself as you mix and match underwear with the people who wear it. You'll be amazed by what an underwear makeover can do. Underwear gives even inanimate objects, such as buildings, plants, and fine art, an instant facelift. This special flip section offers hours of underwear fun for you and your family, and it may inspire a whole new underwearable you. Flip the pages forward and backward—but don't flip your lid!

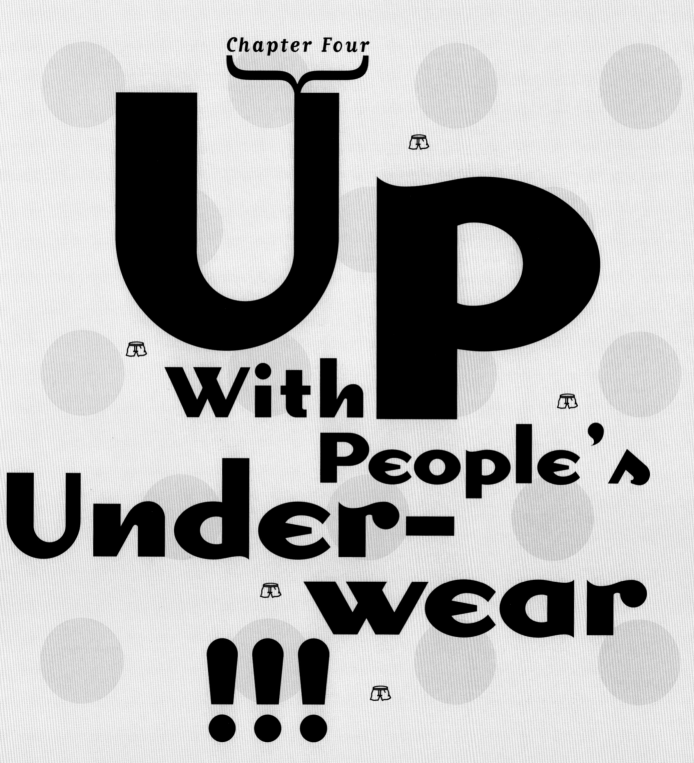

Chapter Four

UP With People's Under-wear!!!

In a perfect world, the facts about underwear care and maintenance would be learned at home. The proper fit of a pair of underwear would be discussed as openly among family members as the fit of shoes, jeans, and gloves. Fathers and sons would go on weekend underwear outings. Mothers would get their children's underwear colors done. Families would march together wearing only underwear in underwear pride parades. And the history of underwear through the ages would be taught in public schools without opposition from fly-by-night underwear oppressors.

But America is not yet an underwear utopia. Consequently, only artists, bohemians, and people living on the fringe of society feel free to debate underwear openly. The typical American suffers from a deep-seated shame, passed down from generation to generation, that keeps him or her from even talking about underwear, much less wearing it with pride in public.

This legacy of underwear denial and shame has eroded the nuclear family and now threatens to stretch to the breaking point the very fiber that holds our society together. Most parents feel awkward and shy about their own underwear and find it difficult to discuss underwear with their children. As a result, America's youth are forced to learn about underwear on the streets or from movies, books and advertisements, which only perpetuate the confusion and misinformation surrounding underwear.

Now is the time to loosen the waistband surrounding our fear and to celebrate underwear's role in our lives. Black or white, rich or poor, tall or short, we all wear underwear. If we are able to talk about it and to promote underwear awareness, together we can put shame behind us.

1953 Boxers in animal prints—leopard, tiger and zebra—become popular.

1955 Elvis Presley performs in briefs.

1956 Elvis Presley performs for the first time in boxer shorts, launching his career and his now-famous swivel-hipped dance.

➤

How to Talk to Your Children About Underwear

It's never too early to begin talking to your children about underwear. The sooner you initiate your child's underwear education, the better your chances of raising a child who is proud of his or her underwear and respectful of underwear diversity.

Most experts agree that children ages five to seven are the most receptive to new ideas. At this age, they are aware of their own underwear but have not yet been socialized to feel embarrassed about it. But each child develops at a different rate, so don't feel you have to wait until a certain age. If your four-year-old boy has begun asking you about the purpose of waistbands or the difference between boxers and briefs, then he is definitely ready for the facts.

Here are some helpful tips for talking to your children about underwear:

☞ Pick a relaxed time when you and your child are free from distractions. Saturday mornings work well.

☞ Use a doll to illustrate how and why underwear is worn.

☞ Encourage your child to ask questions.

☞ Make learning about underwear fun. Wear it on your head. Put a pair on your dog or cat. (Underwear is important but shouldn't be too serious or scary.)

☞ Even if you only wear one type of underwear in your home, be sure to explain that underwear comes in many different sizes, colors, and styles.

Recommended children's books about underwear:

🩲 *Are You My Underwear?*

🩲 *Make Way for Underwear*

🩲 *Underwear the Wild Things Are*

🩲 *Goodnight Underwear*

🩲 *Where's Waldo's Underwear?*

Before going out to shop for underwear, make a list of your underwear needs. Note your waist size and any other distinguishing physical attributes that may affect the way your underwear fits. Most underwear, regardless of the style, will shrink slightly. Make allowances for shrinkage of a quarter to a half inch in the waist and length. Don't be hopeful about sizing—buy the size that fits today. If you lose those extra few pounds, reward yourself later with a smaller size.

Be aware of any allergies to certain fabrics or materials, and be sure to read the label for fabric content before making a purchase. Remember, underwear cannot be returned once opened.

In addition to knowing your size, ask yourself some basic questions. Try to be realistic about your underwear expectations. Even the best pair of underwear can't help you overcome your shortcomings.

Be sure to wear underwear when you go out shopping. If surrounded by a wide selection of sizes and styles when you're craving a pair, you may panic and make a huge impulse purchase that you'll regret once you get home.

If you still have doubts about the right style and size for you, take the underwear personality quiz at right.

- Am I a hang-loose kind of guy or more self-contained?
- Does my work require a wide range of motion?
- What kinds of activities will I be performing in my underwear?
- Will I be seen in my underwear by others?
- Do I plan to use my underwear as an accessory, such as a pocket scarf or ascot?
- Am I left-handed or right-handed?
- Do I work around heavy machinery?
- Do I often wear white polyester pants?
- How do I feel about panty lines and scrunching?
- Do I have easy access to a bathroom during the day?

10 Ways to Show Your Underwear Pride

If you suffer from underwear shame, the first step in working through it is accepting that you have a problem. Once you've done that, you'll make quick progress. Here are 10 fun, easy ways to celebrate your underwear and help you overcome any lingering shame:

❶ Each morning stand in front of a mirror in your underwear and repeat out loud, "I love myself, I love my shorts."

❷ On federal holidays, run a pair of shorts up your flagpole instead of a flag.

❸ Join or start an underwear support group in your neighborhood.

❹ Set aside an hour each week to discuss underwear with your loved ones.

❺ Give underwear as a gift.

❻ Keep a picture of your underwear on your desk at work.

❼ Laugh about underwear whenever possible.

❽ Make friends with people who are more comfortable with underwear than you are.

❾ Work the word "underwear" into conversations at least five times a day.

❿ Look for positive underwear role models in the arts, business, and sports.

In schools across America, young students stand in recognition of the importance of underwear, honoring its role in the continued success of our fine nation.

 1960 The wonder of textile technology gives us more synthetic fabrics, leading to bikini briefs and thongs of mesh and stretch nylon.

1964 Man stays afloat for 17 hours after a boating accident off the coast of Florida thanks to gas trapped in his boxers.

1969 Hundreds of thousands of young Americans gather for a sit-in to protest a pending law banning psychedelic underwear. ➤

Selecting the right size of underwear just isn't enough for today's man. The type of underwear you wear reflects your personality and enhances your lifestyle. What is your underwear personality? Take the following quiz to determine if you should be wearing white briefs, boxers shorts, bikini briefs, boxer briefs, a thong, or no underwear at all.

1. Your waist size is:

a. 28 to 32

b. 34 to 38

c. Constantly changing

d. Less than triple your shoe size

2. The relationship you have with your underwear is best described as:

a. Warm, supportive, caring

b. Adversarial

c. Relaxed and friendly

d. One in which you feel dominated, manipulated, controlled

3. You're most comfortable wearing:

a. A three-piece suit

b. Khakis and a dress shirt

c. Jeans and a T-shirt

d. Your mother's pink Chanel suit

4. At a party where you know only the host, you:

a. Ask him to introduce you to a few other guests

b. Approach someone who looks bored and strike up a conversation on Rush Limbaugh

c. Make yourself useful by washing dishes or passing hors d'oeuvres

d. Get drunk

5. In college, you belonged to:

a. A Fraternity

b. The Communist Party

c. The ultimate Frisbee team

d. A frequent flyer program

6. Your bathroom reading material is most likely:

a. *Sports Illustrated*

b. *The Wall Street Journal*

c. *Mad Magazine*

d. *Martha Stewart Living*

7. Your father wears:

a. Boxer shorts

b. Briefs

c. You don't know, you've never seen him in his underwear

8. The last time you went on a business trip, you:

a. Lost your luggage

b. Had a fling with someone you met in the hotel bar

c. Wore the same pair of underwear for three days

d. Locked yourself out of your hotel room wearing only your underwear

9. In a typical week, you spend the most time sitting:

a. At a desk

b. In traffic

c. At a computer

d. In front of a television

10. I would rather _____ than do my own laundry:

a. Buy all new clothes

b. Sleep with someone I can't stand because they own a washer and dryer

c. Visit my parents for the weekend

d. Not wear underwear

11. You are sexiest:

a. Completely naked

b. Wearing just your underwear

c. Fully clothed

d. Over the phone

12. You identify most with:

a. Tom Jones

b. RuPaul

c. Arnold Schwarzenegger

d. Pee Wee Herman

1970 The Piqua, Ohio, Men's Underwear Drill Team spells out "Merry Christmas" before the big game against North Central High.

1973 Disposable paper underpants go on sale, but not for long.

1975 Jim Palmer and other professional athletes model in underwear advertisements, making briefs sexy business. ➤

69

Scoring	1.	a-0	b-1	c-2	d-6	7.	a-0	b-4	c-6	
	2.	a-2	b-3	c-1	d-6	8.	a-2	b-3	c-0	d-6
	3.	a-3	b-1	c-6	d-0	9.	a-3	b-2	c-4	d-0
	4.	a-1	b-0	c-4	d-5	10.	a-2	b-1	c-0	d-4
	5.	a-0	b-3	c-6	d-4	11.	a-6	b-5	c-2	d-0
	6.	a-1	b-2	c-6	d-3	12.	a-3	b-4	c-1	d-6

12 points or fewer: It's difficult for you to strike a balance between satisfying your adventurous impulses and your increasing need for security. You tend to swing too far to one extreme and everything falls out of balance. Go with bikini briefs. They'll give you the freedom you crave and the support you need to feel centered.

13 to 24 points: Hey Tarzan, you're a swinger! No Jane will ever be able to tame the beast that roars in your jungle. Only the call of the wild can make you purr. Obviously, your natural selection is the thong.

25 to 35 points: You live in the house of half-moon rising and you're ruled by Taurus, the bull. Since your career is filled with financial pressure, you need a relationship that is soft, supportive and caring. White briefs are your best bet .

36 to 47 points: Your shooting star is always on the rise, often setting off fire works around you. Your physical strength comes from the rare Moon-Venus-Mars-Saturn alignment. Only boxer-briefs will give you the social excitement you can't live without.

48 to 59 points: Your list of attributes is long and you have the planetary ruler to prove it. But your power source requires freedom of movement or else financial worries will cramp your style. You're definitely a boxer short man.

60 to 67 points: Nothing holds you back or ties you down. You're always on the move and especially happy when you feel the wind in your hair. The only change you need is a change of perspective. No underwear for you, dude.

68 or more points: You cheated. (The highest possible score is 67.) You're probably wearing underwear on your head, and it's cutting off the circulation to your brain. Remove the underwear and take the quiz again.

How to Store Your Underwear

Unfortunately, most people keep their underwear stuffed in a dark drawer, usually wedged between old sweat socks, with at most a cedar block to spice up their days off. But underwear deserves better treatment.

Think about where your underwear goes to work: inside a pair of pants, where it's dark, hot, stuffy, and often damp from perspiration. And that's on a good day. During a typical work day—often 20 hours long—your underwear is sat on, leaned against, scratched, tugged, and pinched.

For best results, store your underwear where they can breathe fresh air, see the light of day, and even enjoy a nice view. Most boxers are happy just hanging out. A hat rack will do nicely for this, or you may want to install an underwear hanging rack in your bedroom or dressing room. Briefs, more conservative by nature, prefer a bit of support. Try fanning them out on a shelf or arranging them on the top of your bureau.

If you must keep your underwear in a drawer, gently roll each pair or stack them neatly to avoid cramping. And be sure to leave the drawer open an inch or two to let in fresh air and light.

Once a month, give your underwear a special treat. Let them sit out for a day on a windowsill with the window slightly ajar. They will feel refreshed and rejuvenated. Remember, if you're kind to your underwear, your underwear will be kind to you.

Frozen Shorts Sealed for Freshness

Underwear will stay fresh for 2 to 3 weeks when stored in air-tight freezer bags.

Fresh Boxers in a Light Syrup

When preserving your underwear, be sure that each pair is fresh and clean before covering with a light syrup and sealing tightly.

The truth is, underwear is always changing, reconfiguring itself imperceptibly, molecule by molecule, struggling to get out of a pinch or tight situation. But even the most resourceful underwear still needs your help for the big job—the daily change.

How to Change Your Underwear

❶ Find a clean, well-lighted, private place.

❷ Remove trousers. Remove shorts and toss into laundry.

❸ Hold clean pair in front of you, gently grasping waistband with both hands. (Be sure that the fly is facing away from you.)

❹ Slowly lower shorts to knee level, bending slightly at the waist.

❺ Step into leg hole on right side of shorts with right foot (lefties may wish to start with the left foot).

❻ Shift weight to right foot and step into left leg hole with left foot (reverse for lefties).

❼ With both feet on floor, pull shorts up firmly, careful to avoid snagging. When waistband rests comfortably at waist level, release.

How to Change Your Underwear in a Motor Vehicle

❶ If the engine is running, be sure that the transmission is in neutral and that the emergency brake is on.

❷ Check the rear-view mirror and both side mirrors for on-coming traffic. Do not signal to other motorists that you are about to change your shorts.

❸ Using a modified three-point turn, rotate your body to the right of the steering wheel.

❹ Hold your shorts directly in front of you and place both legs into the shorts.

❺ Pull shorts up quickly, being careful not to exceed the posted speed limit.

Warning: If you are intoxicated, do not attempt to change your underwear in a motor vehicle. Ask a sober passenger to change them for you. Remember, friends don't let friends change drunk.

1977 The popularity of tight, white polyester pants causes men to be concerned about visible panty lines (VPL). White, polyester bikini briefs become the rage among the fashionable disco set.

1981 Nobel Prize–winner Mother Teresa holds a press conference to deny allegations that she wears men's briefs on her head. ➥

How to Change Your Underwear in Flight

❶ In preparation for take-off, be sure that no one is watching and that your tray table is safely stowed. Remove old underwear.

❷ Ensure that your legs are in the upright, locked position and that your seat belt is not fastened.

❸ See that both legs are available for insertion into the fresh shorts.

❹ Immediately extinguish all cigarettes.

❺ Hold your shorts in front of you and place one leg into the shorts and then the other, making sure that the lower half of your body is not stowed in the seat-back pocket in front of you.

❻ Pull shorts up firmly, taking care not to place them over your nose and mouth.

Warning: Do not attempt to insert both legs at the same time as this may result in falling over and an oxygen mask may be required. Passengers traveling with children are advised to ask them to be quiet and keep still. In the event of an emergency, lights are unlikely to illuminate. But if they do, go with the flow. You are indeed a lucky man.

How to Change Your Underwear at the Dinner Table

❶ Be sure to compliment the host or hostess on the meal.

❷ Unfold your napkin and place it over your lap.

❸ Discreetly drop a choice piece of meat to the floor to distract any nearby pets.

❹ Hold shorts in front of you under the table, then ask your dining companion a question that will require a long and detailed response.

❺ Maintain a relaxed yet interested expression on your face as you place one leg and then the other into the shorts. If necessary, spill your beverage.

Warning: If you mistake your shorts for your napkin, you may be asked to leave the table.

If Changing Someone Else's Underwear

In the past few years, laws covering the changing of underwear have been significantly modified. Before attempting to change someone else's underwear, you must obtain the other person's permission. It's not enough to assume that the other person wants their underwear changed simply because they are holding a fresh pair. In most states, verbal permission is sufficient to protect you from any liability, but in some states, such as Iowa, Connecticut, and Utah, written permission is required. Check the current laws in your state to avoid a citizen's arrest by a member of the underwear police.

It's easy and fun training your underwear to do things such as to sit, stay, or fetch the newspaper. Underwear learns in a very simple way. Start to train your underwear as soon as you get it home, but keep the lessons short. Try one-minute training sessions frequently throughout the day. In no time, your friends won't believe their eyes when they see what your underwear can do.

1. Teach Your Underwear to Sit

Each time your underwear sits down, say the word "sit" slowly and clearly. While seated, repeat "sit" over and over. Soon your underwear will learn to sit every time you do.

2. Teach Your Underwear to Stay

Hold your hand out flat toward your underwear. Say "stay" slowly and firmly. Then gradually take your hand away, repeating "stay." If your underwear starts to rise, begin again.

3. Teach Your Underwear to Rest at Your Feet

There are times when you want your underwear to rest quietly at your feet. After lowering your underwear around your ankles, repeat the words "lie down." Make sure it doesn't jump up. New underwear leaping up to your face may be fun, but when it gets older, it could knock you over and hurt you.

4. Praise and Reward Your Underwear Immediately

Whenever your underwear does as you've asked, always praise it by saying "good boy" in a friendly tone. New underwear doesn't have a long memory and soon forgets what it has done. One of the best rewards is a warm hug, showing that you love it and appreciate its hard work. Stroke your underwear and talk to it in a loving tone. Or take your underwear for a walk, since it loves to be outdoors, or let it play with a favorite toy.

1985 Men's underwear comes out thanks to pop singer Madonna.

1988 Sexy Calvin Klein advertisements revitalize underwear as a fashion item for men.

1990 Weekend warriors go crazy for athletic-style Lycra briefs. ➤

5. Discipline Your Underwear

If you catch your underwear being naughty, simply say "no" in a loud voice. This is not the time to play with your underwear. Your underwear may look sad, but don't give in. To show that you're angry, don't look at your underwear or touch it. If your underwear continues to misbehave, put it away for a short time. Never, ever strike or use foul language when disciplining your underwear.

<u>Underwear Do's and Don'ts</u>

Do

Select underwear that covers your privates

Treat your underwear as you would like to be treated

Expose your underwear to art

Recycle your underwear

Have a different pair of underwear for every mood

Change your underwear daily

Wash with a gentle detergent in the delicate cycle

Develop a personal rapport with your underwear

Line-dry your underwear whenever possible

Exercise your underwear

Give underwear at birthdays, holidays, anniversaries, and bar mitzvahs

Mention your underwear in your will

Vacation with your underwear

Always wear underwear to family get-togethers

Use your underwear to make friends and influence people

Teach your underwear not to get into a car with strangers

Write off your charitable underwear donations

Talk to your children about underwear

Talk to your underwear

Keep a spare pair in your trunk

Report domestic underwear abuse

Join an underwear support group

Entertain with your underwear

Don't

Lend underwear to friends or family

Leave your underwear unattended in an airport

Buy contraband underwear

Use your underwear as a flotation device

Leave your underwear for long periods in a hot car, even if you've cracked a window

Use underwear as a contraceptive device

Abandon your underwear along the highway

Use your underwear as kindling

Abuse your underwear or violate it in any way

Freeze-dry your underwear

Use your underwear to conceal a dangerous weapon

Smuggle underwear out of a foreign country

Mix prescription drugs and underwear

Use your underwear to hail a cab

Use your underwear for bait

Operate heavy machinery in your underwear

Let your underwear join a gang

Underwear has very simple needs. It likes to be kept warm and dry, it enjoys outdoor exercise, and it should be cleaned on a regular basis. Every pair of underwear needs to know it has a place in your family, so give your underwear a name and make sure it has a safe spot all its own somewhere in your home.

Underwear should be washed after each wearing with a gentle but firm detergent. Most styles can be machine-washed and either tumble- or line-dried. More delicate models require hand-washing. (Be sure to read the manufacturer's instructions regarding bleach.)

Hand-washing tools:

- Mild detergent
- Soft scrub brush
- Plastic tub

Cotton and blends:

- Wash in hot water
- Machine-dry on warm setting
- Cotton retains its shape better when machine-dried, but avoid the hot setting, as over-drying weakens the elasticity of your waistband

Nylon:

- Wash in warm water on delicate cycle
- Dry on the warm, never hot, setting or your underwear may melt
- Nylon will last longer if washed by hand and line-dried

Silk:

- Hand-wash in warm water with Woolite
- Line-dry

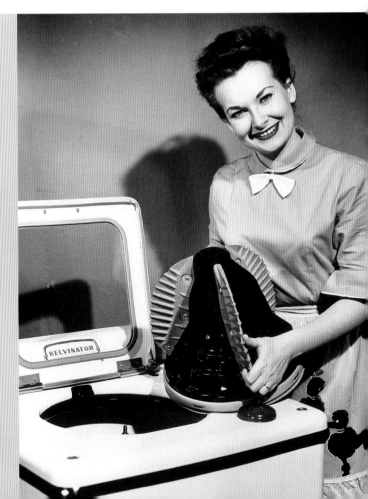

At Home

In the Car

20 Places to Stash An Extra Pair

Even the best of men have days when they just don't feel fresh. But don't let dirty shorts sap your confidence. Take the time to prepare for such days by hiding a few pairs of underwear in places you frequent. A quick change could be the difference between making or breaking that big deal.

At Home

Folded neatly into your VCR

Floating in the toilet tank, in a zip-lock bag

In a can of tennis balls in the hall closet

In the freezer in an empty container of frozen orange juice

In a ceramic vase filled with flowers, in a zip-lock bag

At the Office

At the bottom of a box of tissue

In a hollowed-out book

Inside the towel dispenser in the men's room

Above the ceiling tiles over your desk

Stuffed inside the roll of paper in the fax machine

In Your Car

In the center of the spare tire in the trunk

Folded inside a hubcap

Hanging from your rear view mirror, scented with pine

Under the hood, wrapped in foil

Stuffed inside a commuter cup stuck onto the dash

Public

Taped inside the top of a postal drop box

In a zip-lock bag in a deserted bird's nest

Underneath the drive-thru pick-up window at a nearby fast-food restaurant

Inside the local free-newspaper dispenser

In a jar behind the pickled herring at the grocery store

1992 Aborigines add belts with beepers to their underwear so they won't miss a call while hunting in the outback.

1996 United States Postal Service introduces a series of commemorative underwear stamps.

77

Chapter Five

Pushing the Under- wear Envelope

Once you've decided to just say no to underwear shame, you're ready to introduce briefs and boxers into other aspects of your life. Start gradually, using underwear for other things in private, such as a bookmark or a shower cap. Over time, really push yourself and the underwear envelope by taking your shorts public—decorate your car or office with underwear, throw a "come as your underwear" party.

By outing your underwear in festive ways, you'll meet lots of other people who celebrate underwear while acting as a positive role model for those who still feel underwear discomfort. And don't be surprised by the sort of magical effect that underwear has on people.

☛

Satin shorts make for a glamorous dust ruffle. Bright floral prints work well for throw pillows.

From the moment you begin incorporating underwear into your everyday life, you'll notice a difference. You'll radiate positive energy that attracts interesting and successful people. Strangers will smile at you on the street. Dogs will stop barking when you pass. You'll make friends and influence people and find parking places in a flash. In fact, the more you surround yourself with underwear, the better you'll feel about yourself and your life. So get into underwear pride and get happy!

Early Drafts of Famous Quotations

"Ask not what your underwear can do for you; ask what you can do for your underwear."*–John F. Kennedy*

"O Romeo, Romeo! Underwear art thou Romeo?" *–Romeo and Juliet* by *William Shakespeare*

"In this world, nothing can be said to be certain but death, taxes and underwear." *–Benjamin Franklin*

"Man does not live by briefs only." *–Moses*

"All's well that covers your end well." *–Anonymous*

"I never met a brief I didn't like." *–Will Rogers*

"Candy is dandy but briefs give relief." *–Ogden Nash*

Decorating with underwear

Decorating with underwear is an easy and affordable way to add a splash of color
and style to your home, office, or car.

Your Home:

Bathroom

- Toilet seat cover
- Hand towels
- Decorative garbage-can liner

Kitchen

- Toaster cover
- Dish towels
- Tea cozy

Living Room

- Throw pillow cover
- Arm rest cover
- Ottoman skirt

Your Office:

- Desk lamp cover
- Rolodex dust cover
- Color-coded file organizers
- Desk blotter
- PC screen protector

Your Car:

- Headrest cover
- Decorative hubcap covers
- Hood ornament
- Steering wheel cover
- Rear-view mirror ornament
- Novelty window toy
- Mud flaps

Entertaining is a great way to share underwear with friends and family, and to turn celebrating underwear into a group activity. Whether you build an entire party around an underwear theme, such as the Underwear Olympics, or simply use underwear as festive accents, be sure to put out the underwear welcome mat for your guests. This not only signifies your underwear pride but also sets the tone for your event.

Popular Underwear Party Themes

Underwear Academy Awards Party

Underwear Tea Party

Underwear Open House

Underwear Engagement Party

Underwear Baby Shower

St. Patrick's Underwear Day Celebration

Underwear Garden Party

Stag Underwear Party

Underwear Singles Mixer

Come as Your Underwear

Underwear Slumber Party

Underwear Entertaining Tips

•If you're serving punch, dress the punch bowl in a pair of large boxer shorts.

•Surprise your guests with individually-wrapped underwear as party favors.

•Instead of using plain old paper, write your invitations on underwear, then mail.

•For sit-down receptions, alternate brief-wearers and boxer-wearers at each table.

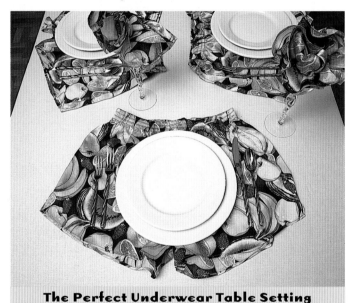

The Perfect Underwear Table Setting

Any good host or hostess knows the importance of an elegant table setting to the success of a dinner party. Entertaining with underwear is no different—the table setting is the stage for your meal and deserves careful planning and execution to ensure a unique dining experience.

•When serving hot hors d'oeuvres, use clean, white briefs instead of doilies on passing trays.

•Make a birthday cake in the shape of the birthday boy's favorite pair.

Underwear Party Games

When gathering a group of people who don't know one another very well, underwear party games can be a terrific ice breaker for children or adults.

Children's Games

- Musical Underwear
- Pin the Underwear on the Donkey
- Kick the Can of Underwear
- Hide and Seek Your Underwear
- Underwear Scavenger Hunt
- Underwear Piñata
- Three-legged Underwear Races

Adult Games

- Truth or Underwear
- Underwear Charades
- Spin the Underwear
- Underwear Origami Contest
- Famous People's Underwear
- Pass the Underwear
- Underwear Trivia

How to Make an Underwear Bouquet for Your Table

You need: six pairs of clean, bright-colored boxer shorts, 36 feet of wire, wire cutters, a large vase

1. Cut wire into six three-foot pieces.
2. Grasp the legs of a pair of shorts firmly in one hand about three inches from the bottom, creating a "blossom."
3. Wrap remaining wire around the base of the "blossom," twist once to secure, then twist the "stem" into a tight spiral and wind the wire down around the base of the "stem."
4. Secure wire at the base.
5. When each underwear flower is complete, arrange all six in a vase and display proudly.

Foolproof Underwear Recipes

As you get to know underwear better, you'll discover that many styles are edible. Experiment with your favorite recipes by simply substituting underwear for other main ingredients. Or, try one of these foolproof underwear recipes.

Fried Brief Tomatoes

4 pairs clean white briefs

4 tablespoons of fresh butter

$1/4$ cup chopped scallions

10 cherry tomatoes, sliced medium

$1/2$ teaspoon salt

$1/4$ teaspoon celery salt

$1/2$ teaspoon pepper

❶ Place briefs in large skillet and sauté in butter with chopped scallions. Add seasoning and tomatoes, stirring often. When briefs are browned, reduce heat, cover and simmer for 20 minutes.

❷ Serve briefs and tomatoes over rice with baby peas.
Serves four

Strawberry Shortscake

2 cups unbleached all-purpose flour

2 tablespoons granulated sugar

2 pairs multicolored shorts, shredded

³/₄ teaspoon salt

1 tablespoon baking powder

4 tablespoons sweet butter, chilled

¹/₂ cup light cream

sweet butter, softened for topping

6 cups strawberries, sliced

1 ¹/₂ cups heavy cream, chilled

12 perfect strawberries (garnish)

❶ Preheat oven to 450 degrees.

❷ Sift flour, sugar, salt, and baking powder together into mixing bowl.

❸ Cut 4 tablespoons butter until mixture resembles oats. Pour in cream and mix gently until just blended.

❹ Fold in shredded shorts.

❺ Roll dough out onto floured work surface to a thickness of ¹/₂ inch. Cut into 3-inch circles with a cookie cutter. Gather scraps, roll again, and cut into more rounds; you should have 6 rounds.

❻ Bake shortscakes on a greased baking sheet for about 10 minutes, or until puffed and lightly browned.

Other suggested dishes:

Brief Stroganoff

Barbecued Shorts Ribs

Brief Burritos

Roasted Free-range Boxers

❼ Cool biscuits slightly, split them, and spread softened butter lightly over the cut surfaces. Set the bottoms on dessert plates; spoon on sliced strawberries. Whip chilled cream, and spoon a dollop onto each shortscake, then garnish with a single perfect strawberry. Serve immediately.

Serves six

Say good-bye to costly health-club memberships, tedious workout videos, and heavy barbells. If you have a good selection of underwear, then you've got everything you need for an at-home underwear workout. Do it by yourself or with a friend—it's safe, easy, and fun!

Each exercise is designed to work a specific muscle group. So go for the burn. But if you experience sharp pain or joint strain at any point, take a break. And remember to drink plenty of water before, during, and after your workout to avoid dehydration and cramping.

Warming up

Place both hands inside the waistband of a pair of shorts. Rotate one hand in a circle twice to twist waistband and hold wrists securely and comfortably in place. Holding arms as straight as possible, circle around head five times. Reverse direction and circle again. With knees slightly bent, lean forward and touch toes with underwear. Raise arms behind head as far as is comfortable and arch back as far as is comfortable for a 10 count. Remove underwear.

Then, throw 10 pairs of underwear up in the air. Gather them one by one with hands, bending at the knees, not the waist. Repeat, but gather each pair one by one with feet, lifting foot up to your hand.

Knee Squeezes

Step into a pair of underwear and pull up to knee-level. With feet wide, bend knees, then bring thighs together and apart, together and apart. Do three sets of 30. For better balance, keep hands at waist.

Leg Lifts

Sit back on the floor and place your hands beside your waist for lower back support. Pick up a pair of underwear between your feet and hold it above the floor with knees bent. Count to 20. Extend legs, hold at a 45° angle, and count to 20. Lift legs straight up, hold, and count to 20. Do five sets.

Neck Builders

Place a pair of large underwear around your neck. Then squat down and secure the underwear under one foot. (The elastic waistband should be taut but not painful on your neck.) Hold head firmly in place as you slowly straighten legs, increasing the pressure on your neck muscles. For an extra challenge, raise your arms overhead and flex. Do a set of 20, rest for 30 seconds, then repeat.

When sharing your underwear with household pets, be sure to choose a size that won't restrict your dog or cat's movement. And be sensitive to your pet's personality. You wouldn't want to embarrass him or her with the wrong style of shorts.

Designer Duds for Dogs

Most dogs are big enough to sport underwear much the way we do—hind legs through the two holes with the waistband worn around their middle. The fly, of course, should be worn on top so that their tails can wag proudly without being restricted.

Snug-fitting briefs are best for breeds with short legs:

- Pekingese
- Basset hound
- Dachshund
- Highland terrier
- Corgi
- Pug

Larger breeds prefer boxer shorts, which not only give them ample room to move but also convey their relaxed, easy-going nature:

- Dalmatian
- Boxer
- German shepherd
- Labrador
- Irish wolfhound
- Great dane
- Mastiff

More exotic breeds, with real moxie and style, wouldn't be caught dead in boxer shorts or plain white briefs. These fashion hounds deserve bikini briefs or a thong to show off their sleek canine lines:

- Whippet
- Doberman
- Afghan hound
- Standard poodle
- Airedale terrier

Fetching Feline Fashions

Despite their independent, aloof nature, cats also like to express themselves with underwear. A cat's delicate feline frame, however, calls for a bit of creative styling.

The Siamese Sarong: Cat's head pokes through fly of briefs with waistband worn over one shoulder.

The Calico Cape: Boxer shorts are wrapped around cat's neck and secured with safety pin.

The Persian Poncho: Cat's head goes through waistband of baggy boxers and then pokes out fly.

The Manx Saddle: Bobbed tail is held snugly in thong with straps worn over front shoulders.

Alternative Uses for Underwear

There are endless uses for boxers or briefs in daily life besides as underwear or briefs. Remember: The possibilities of underwear are limited only by your imagination.

Blank check • Semaphore flags • Coffee filter
Pot holders • Sling for sprained arm • Book mark
Hand towel for golf bag • Gift-wrapping paper
Bird-cage cover • Personalized luggage identifier
Lunch bag • Shower cap • Note paper
TV tray tablecloth • Basketball hoop net
Tennis racket cover • Butterfly net •
Flour sifter • Ice pack • Wind sock

Accessorizing with Underwear

As you become more comfortable with underwear, try accessorizing with a splashy pair of boxers or briefs. A man who wears his underwear as a pocket square or necktie exudes a unique sense of style, confidence, and humor. And don't be afraid to take underwear formal. Silk boxer shorts add real panache to a traditional black tuxedo. For more casual affairs, wear your underwear as an ascot or festive headwear. And if you really want to distinguish yourself from the pack, cover your motorcycle helmet with a pair of brightly colored bikini briefs.

Underwear as outerwear:
Necktie • Ascot • Cummerbund
Pocket square • Hats and headwear
Motorcycle helmet cover

If you have a problem with underwear or would like to help others who do, there are a variety of established organizations to contact. Check your local phone directory to find a chapter near you, or call one of their national hotlines for more information.

Green Briefs

An international action group dedicated to protecting the underwear environment.

People for the Ethical Treatment of Underwear (PETU)

Dedicated to raising public awareness of underwear rights and enforcing proper treatment of underwear.

Stay Up!

An underground group of political activists promoting underwear pride and fund-raising for underwear research.

Underwear Abusers Anonymous (UAA)

A national support group that provides individual and group counseling for underwear abusers.

Underwearers Anonymous (UA)

For those who realize that they are addicted to and powerless over underwear.

The Association of Free-Range Underwear Growers

Underwear professionals practicing and promoting humane underwear farming.

BADD (Brothers Against Double Duty)

An international organization fighting to end two-day underwear abuse.

The Fresh-Air Underwear Fund

Providing summer outings in the country to underprivileged, inner-city underwear.

United Coalition of Underwear Aromatherapists

A scientific research group exploring the frontier of healing through underwear aromas.

If You're Considering a Professional Career in Underwear

The underwear industry, one of the most competitive in the world of fashion, attracts thousands of talented people each year. The demands are rigorous—long hours, short shorts, constant change—and the end is always at hand. Only the best and the brightest survive, much less make a name for themselves.

If you're considering a professional career in underwear, first answer these questions:

1. Are you worthy?
2. Is your head in your pants?
3. Do you uphold the ideals of underwear?
4. Are you focused on the bottom line?
5. Do you dream about underwear?
6. Can you handle intense pressure in your underwear?
7. Is underwear as important to you as shoes?
8. At a party, do you always work the conversation back to underwear?
9. Have you ever smoked underwear? If so, did you inhale?
10. Do you frequently have unholy thoughts about underwear?

If you've answered yes to all these questions then you may have what it takes to make it in underwear. For more information contact:

Allied Underwear Association
100 East 42nd Street
New York, NY 10017

National Underwear Association
136 West 41st Street
New York, NY 10036

Underwear-Negligee Associates
100 East 42nd Street
New York, NY 10017

National Knitwear Manufacturers Association
(formerly the Underwear Institute)
365 South Street
Morristown, NJ 07960

RECIPE OF THE WEEK ···· **KABOBS** ····

KABOBS

- - - - - - - -

52 EASY RECIPES FOR YEAR-ROUND GRILLING

SALLY SAMPSON

PHOTOGRAPHY BY YUNHEE KIM

BICENTENNIAL
1807
WILEY
2007
BICENTENNIAL

JOHN WILEY & SONS, INC.

Published by John Wiley & Sons, Inc., Hoboken, New Jersey
Published simultaneously in Canada

For general information about our other products and services, please contact our Customer Care Department within the United States at (800) 762-2974, outside the United States at (317) 572-3993 or fax (317) 572-4002. Wiley also publishes its books in a variety of electronic formats. Some content that appears in print may not be available in electronic books. For more information about Wiley products, visit our web site at www.wiley.com.

BOOK DESIGN BY DEBORAH KERNER / DANCING BEARS
PHOTOGRAPHY COPYRIGHT © 2007 BY YUNHEE KIM
FOOD STYLING BY JEE LEVIN
PROP STYLING BY DEBORAH WILLIAMS

Library of Congress Cataloging-in-Publication Data:

Sampson, Sally, 1955-
    Recipe of the week : kabobs / Sally Sampson.
        p. cm.
    Includes index.
    ISBN-13: 978-0-471-92140-0 (pbk.)
    1. Skewer cookery. I. Title.
    TX834.S26 2007
    741.7'6--dc22

                            2006025133

Printed in the China
10 9 8 7 6 5 4 3 2

Acknowledgments

My thanks to all who contributed to this book
by offering recipes for kabobs, eating kabobs,
and thinking about kabobs, kabobs and
more kabobs.

and my delicious
and wonderful children,
Lauren and Ben,
and Nancy, especially Zach
and always Carla.

Contents

• • • • • • • • ▶ • introduction

When I started cooking in my 20's, I imagined I would discover a perfect cookbook and cook through every recipe, from start to finish, canapés to desserts. Maybe, I thought, I'd do it on weekends. Maybe nightly. I never did cook through a cookbook, not because there aren't a million great cookbooks out there—because, in fact, there are. But I found that when I tackled one kind of recipe—say, kabobs—once I achieved a certain level of mastery, I wanted to just keep on going. I wanted to try every kind of kabob.

So instead of cooking through a cookbook, I've cooked into a cookbook: 52 kabobs. One kabob a week for a year. **Kebab, kabob, shish kebbab, shashlik, kebap or kabab.** Whatever you call those little pieces of meat that are skewered, marinated (usually) and grilled, they seem to span every ethnic cuisine and almost every course. When I started writing this book, someone asked me if it wasn't silly to write a whole book on kabobs. I can say, with total certainty, having eaten kabobs almost every night month after month, that it is not in the least bit silly. Every kind of meat, fish and poultry and almost every vegetable and fruit can be skewered and the possibilities are endless. Additionally, kabobs include almost all food groups, and when served with rice, result in a perfect meal. Kabobs are more fun than slabs of meat and are easy enough to make on weekdays and yet special enough for a party. Although **52 kabobs** may seem daunting, just think: **it's only one a week.**

And have fun skewering!

Tips on Grilling

I grill year-round (sometimes in snow boots and a hat) and always use a charcoal chimney starter, which can be purchased at most hardware stores. Most importantly, you don't need charcoal fluid. You simply fill the bottom of the chimney with two pieces of crumpled newspaper and the top with hardwood lump charcoal. Light the newspaper and burn until the coals are glowing red, 15 to 20 minutes. Dump the coals out into the bottom of the grill and, using tongs, spread them out evenly. Cover with the grate.

After 5 minutes, use a wire brush to thoroughly clean the grate. When the coals are covered with a pale gray ash and you can leave your hand 5 inches above the fire for 2 to 3 seconds, the coals are ready.

Tips on Skewers

I don't recommend the thin wooden sticks that are sold everywhere for two reasons. When you put food on them, the food tends to spin around when you turn it, resulting in some sides cooking twice while others don't cook at all. Additionally, the skewers themselves burn. Common wisdom is that in order to prevent the wooden skewers from burning, you should soak them in water for anywhere from 20 minutes to 2 hours. I haven't found that soaking for any amount of time makes a difference: the part of the skewer that isn't completely covered with ingredients burns, and unless you are serving the meats off the skewer, the burnt edges ruin the fun (of eating off a skewer) and the presentation.

I prefer skewers that are flat, like long metal Popsicle sticks, or double-pronged, like a long metal or wooden bobby pin. If these aren't available, simply double skewer the food with thin metal skewers by putting 2 skewers through the meat.

Essential Equipment

Microplane grater

Skewers

8-inch chef's knife

Brush

Reamer

Juicer

Grill

3-quart glass or ceramic bowl

Tongs

Charcoal chimney starter

Heavy duty oven mitts

Wire brush, for cleaning the grill grate

> • the recipes

Beef with Toasted Sesame Oil, Soy and Cilantro ● ● ● ● ● ● ● ● ● ● ● ● ●

SERVES 6

Although this marinade includes soy sauce, it's the toasted sesame oil that gives this dish a decidedly Asian flavor. Don't think of substituting regular sesame oil: the sesame seeds in toasted sesame oil have been toasted first, which gives the oil a much stronger and wonderfully smoky (but occasionally bitter) taste. Toasted sesame oil should be used in small quantities whereas regular sesame oil, which is made directly from fresh sesame seeds (and tastes just like sesame seeds) is more mellow, making it ideal for salad dressing.

Serve with steamed rice, a crunchy salad of romaine lettuce with oranges and lightly toasted walnuts and/or grilled asparagus. Add lightly oiled broccoli, zucchini and bell peppers to the skewers.

½ cup low sodium soy sauce

½ cup chopped fresh cilantro leaves

2 tablespoons toasted sesame oil

2 garlic cloves, minced

2 teaspoons ground cumin

½ teaspoon crushed red pepper flakes

3 pounds sirloin tips, left in long, thin strips, or top blade steaks, trimmed of fat and cut into 1¼-inch cubes

1 teaspoon kosher salt

½ teaspoon freshly ground black pepper

To make the marinade: Place the soy sauce, cilantro, sesame oil, garlic, cumin and red pepper flakes in a non-reactive 3- to 4-quart bowl and mix until all the ingredients are well combined. Add the beef to the bowl and mix until it is completely immersed in the marinade. Alternatively, you can transfer the mixture to a large resealable plastic bag. Refrigerate for at least 4 hours and up to overnight.

Prepare a grill. When the coals are glowing red, after 15 to 20 minutes, cover with the grate. After 5 minutes, use a wire brush to thoroughly clean the grate. When the

continued on next page

coals are covered with a pale gray ash and you can leave your hand 5 inches above the fire for 2 seconds, the coals are ready.

To cook, remove as much marinade as possible from the beef. Thread the beef on skewers and sprinkle all sides with the salt and pepper. Place the kabobs on the grate and grill, turning every 1½ minutes, until the beef is deeply browned on the outside and rare in the inside, 8 to 10 minutes total. Transfer to a serving platter and serve immediately.

Zach Demuth's Tofu Satay ● ● ● ● ● ●

SERVES 6

Zach Demuth helps me with my cookbooks, doing this and that. Lucky for me, he went to the Chiang Mai Cooking School in Chiangmai, Thailand, last summer and brought back this wonderful recipe.

Generally, says Zach, it's served as an appetizer before chicken/potato red curry and sticky rice. I like it so much, I eat it for a main course, also with sticky rice.

2 cups unsweetened coconut milk

2½ tablespoons fish sauce (or 1½ tablespoons
    soy sauce for vegetarians)

1½ tablespoons canola oil

¼ cup sugar

1 generous tablespoon yellow curry powder

1½ pounds extra firm tofu, cut into long narrow
    strips, about ¾-inch thick

To make the marinade: Place the coconut milk, fish sauce, canola oil, sugar and curry powder in a 3- to 4-quart bowl and mix until all the ingredients are well combined. Add the tofu to the bowl and mix until it is completely immersed in the marinade. Alternatively, you can transfer the mixture to a large resealable plastic bag. Refrigerate for at least 15 minutes and up to 1 hour.

Prepare a grill. When the coals are glowing red, after 15 to 20 minutes, cover with the grate. After 5 minutes, use a wire brush to thoroughly clean the grate. When the coals are covered with a pale gray ash and you can leave your hand 5 inches above the fire for 2 to 3 seconds, the coals are ready.

To cook, remove as much marinade as possible from the tofu. Thread the tofu on the skewers, place the kabobs on the grate and grill, turning once, until the tofu is golden brown and just firm, about 3 minutes per side. Transfer to a serving platter and serve immediately.

Asian Shrimp ● ● ● ● ● ● ● ● ● ● ●

SERVES 6

Another great condiment to have on hand, hoisin sauce (also called Peking sauce) adds a wonderful sweet and spicy flavor to this marinade. Made from fermented soybeans, sugar, garlic and vinegar, it is a thick red-brown sauce that is most often used in Chinese cuisine.

Serve these kabobs with steamed rice and broccoli. Add bell peppers and red onions to the skewer.

2 tablespoons low sodium soy sauce

2 tablespoons hoisin sauce

2 tablespoons toasted sesame oil

2 tablespoons unseasoned rice vinegar

2 teaspoons chili paste with garlic

36 large peeled deveined shrimp, about
   1¼ pounds

1 lemon or lime, cut into 6 wedges

To make the marinade: Place the soy sauce, hoisin sauce, toasted sesame oil, rice vinegar and chili paste in a non-reactive 3- to 4-quart bowl and mix until all the ingredients are well combined. Add the shrimp to the bowl and mix until it is completely immersed in the marinade. Alternatively, you can transfer the mixture to a large resealable plastic bag. Refrigerate for at least 2 hours and up to 4 hours.

Prepare a grill. When the coals are glowing red, after 15 to 20 minutes, cover with the grate. After 5 minutes, use a wire brush to thoroughly clean the grate. When the coals are covered with a pale gray ash and you can leave your hand 5 inches above the fire for 2 to 3 seconds, the coals are ready.

To cook, remove as much marinade as possible from the shrimp. Thread the shrimp on the skewers, place the kabobs on the grate and grill, turning once, until the shrimp are golden brown and firm, about 2 minutes per side. Transfer to a serving platter and serve immediately, garnished with the lemon or lime.

Chicken Strips with Peanut Sauce ● ● ●

A classic Thai-inspired kabob; these are great as an appetizer. The sauce is also good for dipping blanched vegetables like broccoli, cauliflower and carrots.

Serve with Chinese or sticky rice.

⅓ cup low sodium soy sauce

⅓ cup seasoned rice wine vinegar

⅓ cup mild oil, such as canola or vegetable or safflower

1 tablespoon minced fresh ginger

3 pounds skinless, boneless chicken breasts or thighs, trimmed of fat and pounded into long strips

Chopped fresh cilantro leaves

Chopped scallion greens

FOR THE PEANUT SAUCE:

¾ cup natural peanut butter (no sugar)

1 cup boiling water

2 tablespoons low sodium soy sauce

2 teaspoons seasoned rice wine vinegar

3 garlic cloves

2 teaspoons sugar

1 teaspoon minced fresh ginger

¼ teaspoon kosher salt

⅛ to ¼ teaspoon cayenne

To make the marinade: Place the soy sauce, rice vinegar, oil and ginger in a non-reactive 3- to 4-quart bowl and mix until all the ingredients are well combined. Add the chicken to the bowl and mix until it is completely immersed in the marinade. Alternatively, you can transfer the mixture to a large resealable plastic bag. Refrigerate for at least 1 hour and up to 3 hours.

While the chicken is marinating, make the Peanut Sauce: Place the peanut butter and boiling water in a food processor fitted with a steel blade and process until the ingredients come together. Gradually, while the processor is running, add the soy sauce, vinegar, garlic, sugar, ginger, salt, and cayenne and process until creamy. Transfer to a container and refrigerate for at least 1 hour and up to 1 week.

Prepare a grill. When the coals are glowing red, after 15 to 20 minutes, cover with the grate. After 5 minutes, use a wire brush to thoroughly clean the grate. When the coals are covered with a pale gray ash and you can leave your hand 5 inches above the fire for 2 to 3 seconds, the coals are ready.

To cook, remove as much marinade as possible from the chicken and thread the chicken on skewers. Place the kabobs on the grate and grill, turning every 1½ minutes, until the chicken is well browned on the outside and no longer pink in the inside, 8 to 10 minutes total. Transfer to a serving platter and serve immediately with the Peanut Sauce on top or on the side. Garnish with chopped cilantro and scallions and serve immediately.

Curried Pork with Coconut and Cilantro ●

Coconut milk is not actually milk at all nor even the liquid that is found inside a coconut. Coconut milk is made from shredded or ground coconut meat mixed with water and then strained to achieve a thick, white liquid. This mixture is then left out so that the fat solids, also known as coconut cream (again, a misnomer), will harden at the top. The remaining liquid is sold in cans as coconut milk. Coconut milk has a strong coconut flavor and is commonly used as a base for curry. Any leftover coconut milk should be covered and refrigerated.

Serve with steamed rice (with or without currants) and cucumbers with thickened yogurt and fresh mint and/or dill. Add lightly oiled zucchini, red onions and mangoes or peaches to the skewer.

½ cup unsweetened coconut milk

¼ cup chopped fresh cilantro leaves, plus
   extra for garnish

2 tablespoons chutney (any kind is fine)

1 tablespoon plus 1 teaspoon curry powder

1½ teaspoons kosher salt

3 pounds pork butt, boneless center cut chops
   or pork shoulder, trimmed of fat and cut
   into 1¼-inch cubes

½ teaspoon freshly ground black pepper

Lightly toasted coconut

Lightly toasted cashews

To make the marinade: Place the coconut milk, cilantro, chutney, curry powder and ½ teaspoon of the salt in a non-reactive 3- to 4-quart bowl and mix until all the ingredients are well combined. Add the pork to the bowl and mix until it is completely immersed in the marinade. Alternatively, you can transfer the mixture to a large resealable plastic bag. Refrigerate for at least 4 hours and up to 8 hours.

Prepare a grill. When the coals are glowing red, after 15 to 20 minutes, cover with the grate. After 5 minutes, use a wire brush to thoroughly clean the grate. When the coals are covered with a pale gray ash and you can leave your hand 5 inches above the fire for 2 to 3 seconds, the coals are ready.

continued on next page

To cook, remove as much marinade as possible from the pork. Thread the pork on skewers and sprinkle all sides with the remaining teaspoon of salt and the pepper. Place the kabobs on the grate and grill, turning every 1½ minutes, until the pork is deeply browned on the outside and medium rare in the inside, 9 to 10 minutes total. Transfer to a serving platter, sprinkle with cilantro, coconut and cashews and serve immediately.

Chicken with Sun-Dried Tomatoes and Basil ● ● ● ● ● ● ● ● ● ● ●

Although I am not a fan of sun-dried tomatoes, I love this rich sauce. Serve these kabobs alongside a green salad with goat cheese and a crusty loaf of bread.

¼ cup olive oil, plus extra for brushing

⅓ cup finely grated Parmesan cheese

3 tablespoons chopped sun-dried tomatoes in oil

3 tablespoons chopped fresh basil leaves

1 large garlic clove

1 teaspoons kosher salt

3 pounds skinless, boneless chicken breasts
   or thighs, trimmed of fat and cut into
   1¼-inch chunks

½ teaspoon freshly ground black pepper

To make the sauce: Place the olive oil, Parmesan cheese, sun-dried tomatoes, basil, garlic and ½ teaspoon of the salt in a food processor fitted with a steel blade and process until thick and creamy. Set aside.

Prepare a grill. When the coals are glowing red, after 15 to 20 minutes, cover with the grate. After 5 minutes, use a wire brush to thoroughly clean the grate. When the coals are covered with a pale gray ash and you can leave your hand 5 inches above the fire for 2 to 3 seconds, the coals are ready.

To cook, brush the chicken with olive oil, then thread on skewers and sprinkle all sides with the remaining ½ teaspoon of salt and the pepper. Place the kabobs on the grate and grill, turning every 1½ minutes, until the chicken is well browned on the outside and no longer pink in the inside, 8 to 10 minutes total. Transfer to a serving platter, drizzle with the Parmesan–Sun-Dried Tomato sauce and serve immediately.

WEEK 6

KABOBS

13

Swordfish with Brown Butter and Chives ● ● ● ● ● ● ● ● ● ● ● ● ●

SERVES 6

Perfect for an elegant dinner party or a romantic dinner for two (in which case divide the recipe by three), these rich nutty kabobs are great with steamed asparagus and a Boston lettuce salad with lemon dressing.

2 tablespoons olive oil	8 tablespoons (1 stick) unsalted butter
3 pounds swordfish steaks, skin removed, meat cut into 1-inch cubes	¼ cup balsamic vinegar
	2 teaspoons Dijon mustard
1½ teaspoons kosher salt	2 tablespoons fresh chives, plus additional
½ teaspoon freshly ground black pepper	for garnish

To make the marinade: Place the olive oil, swordfish, salt and pepper in a non-reactive 3- to 4-quart bowl and mix until the swordfish is well coated. Alternatively, you can transfer the mixture to a large resealable plastic bag. Cover and refrigerate 3 to 4 hours.

While the fish marinates, place the butter in a small saucepan over low heat and cook, stirring occasionally, until it just begins to foam and is well browned but not burnt, about 5 minutes. Add the balsamic vinegar and cook until it thickens somewhat, about 3 minutes. Add the mustard and chives and cook 2 additional minutes. Set aside until ready to use.

Prepare a grill. When the coals are glowing red, after 15 to 20 minutes, cover with the grate. After 5 minutes, use a wire brush to thoroughly clean the grate. When the coals are covered with a pale gray ash and you can leave your hand 5 inches above the fire for 2 to 3 seconds, the coals are ready.

To cook, thread the swordfish on skewers, place the kabobs on the grate and grill, turning every 1½ minutes, until the swordfish is well browned on the outside but still rare in the inside, 7 to 8 minutes total. Transfer to a serving platter, drizzle with the brown butter sauce and serve immediately, garnished with additional chives.

Hoisin Sesame Pork ● ● ● ● ● ● ● ●

SERVES 6

I have to admit that when a recipe calls for rice wine vinegar, I never know whether to use unseasoned or seasoned so I have hedged and called for mildly seasoned. Usually labeled as "rice vinegar," rice wine vinegar is made from Chinese rice wine, which tastes similar to dry sherry or vermouth. It comes in three varieties: red, black, and the most commonly used, white, most often used in sushi rice. When seasoned, it includes salt, pepper, garlic, and occasionally red chili flakes, which makes it a good choice for salad dressing.

Steamed rice and a green like snow peas, broccoli or asparagus are the perfect accompaniments for this Asian-inspired dish.

½ cup low sodium soy sauce

2 tablespoons toasted sesame oil

2 tablespoons mildly seasoned rice vinegar

2 tablespoons hoisin sauce

6 scallions, trimmed and minced

3 garlic cloves, minced

3 pounds pork butt, boneless center cut chops or pork shoulder, trimmed of fat and cut into 1¼-inch cubes

2 tablespoons toasted sesame seeds (see Note) and/or ¼ cup chopped roasted peanuts

To make the marinade: Place the soy sauce, sesame oil, rice vinegar, hoisin, scallions and garlic in a non-reactive 3- to 4-quart bowl and mix until all the ingredients are well combined. Add the pork to the bowl and mix until it is completely immersed in the marinade. Alternatively, you can transfer the mixture to a large resealable plastic bag. Refrigerate for at least 4 hours and up to 8 hours.

Prepare a grill. When the coals are glowing red, after 15 to 20 minutes, cover with the grate. After 5 minutes, use a wire brush to thoroughly clean the grate. When the coals are covered with a pale gray ash and you can leave your hand 5 inches above the fire for 2 to 3 seconds, the coals are ready.

To cook, remove as much marinade as possible from the pork. Thread the pork on the skewers. Place the kabobs on the grate and grill, turning every 1½ minutes, until

continued on next page

the pork is deeply browned on the outside and medium rare in the inside, 9 to 10 minutes total. Transfer to a serving platter, sprinkle with sesame seeds and/or peanuts and serve immediately.

NOTE • TO TOAST SEEDS OR NUTS: Preheat the oven to 300°F. Place the seeds or nuts in a single layer on a dry baking sheet. Transfer to the oven and bake until golden brown, 10 to 12 minutes. Set aside to cool and proceed with recipe.

Smoked Paprika Chicken ● ● ● ● ● ● ●

SERVES 6

Spanish smoked paprika is an amazing treat. Made from peppers that have been smoke-dried over oak wood, it is also called pimenton. Not widely available but worth searching high and low for, Spanish smoked paprika is usually found in chorizo, paella and marinades for meat. Spanish smoked paprika is very different from Hungarian, which should never be considered a substitute. It is sold in three forms: dulce/sweet (deep smoky flavor and slightly sweet), agridulce/semisweet (oaky, smoky and bitter) and picante/hot (smoky and bitter). Look for brands that come from La Vera, where the climate produces the highest quality Spanish paprika. Serve with spaetzle and cauliflower: roasted, mashed, or raw with dressing.

3 tablespoons olive oil

3 tablespoons fresh lemon juice

3 tablespoons fresh Italian flat leaf parsley leaves

2 tablespoons smoked paprika

1 tablespoon fresh rosemary leaves or
   $\frac{1}{2}$ tablespoon dried

$1\frac{1}{2}$ teaspoons kosher salt

3 pounds skinless, boneless chicken breasts
   or thighs, trimmed of fat and cut into
   $1\frac{1}{4}$-inch chunks

$\frac{1}{2}$ teaspoon freshly ground black pepper

1 lemon, cut into 6 wedges

To make the marinade: Place the olive oil, lemon juice, parsley, paprika, rosemary and $\frac{1}{2}$ teaspoon of the salt in a non-reactive 3- to 4-quart bowl and mix until all the ingredients are well combined. Add the chicken to the bowl and mix until it is completely covered with the paste. Alternatively, you can transfer the mixture to a large resealable plastic bag. Refrigerate for at least 4 hours and up to 8 hours.

Prepare a grill. When the coals are glowing red, after 15 to 20 minutes, cover with the grate. After 5 minutes, use a wire brush to thoroughly clean the grate. When the coals are covered with a pale gray ash and you can leave your hand 5 inches above the fire for 2 to 3 seconds, the coals are ready.

To cook, remove as much paste as possible from the chicken. Thread the chicken on skewers and sprinkle all sides with the remaining teaspoon of salt and the pepper. Place the kabobs on the grate and grill, turning every $1\frac{1}{2}$ minutes, until the chicken is well browned on the outside and no longer pink in the inside, 8 to 10 minutes total. Transfer to a serving platter and serve immediately, garnished with the lemon.

Spicy Shrimp with Olive Oil and Parsley ● ● ● ● ● ● ● ● ● ● ● ●

SERVES 6

This very basic, very easy shrimp kabob is great with almost any green vegetable and garlic bread.

¼ cup olive oil

¼ cup chopped Italian flat leaf parsley leaves

3 garlic cloves, minced

3 small chile peppers, chopped

1½ teaspoons kosher salt

36 large peeled deveined shrimp, about 1¼ pounds

½ teaspoon freshly ground black pepper

1 lemon, cut into 6 wedges

To make the marinade: Place the olive oil, parsley, garlic, chile peppers and ½ teaspoon of the salt in a non-reactive 3- to 4-quart bowl and mix until all the ingredients are well combined. Add the shrimp to the bowl and mix until it is completely immersed in the marinade. Alternatively, you can transfer the mixture to a large resealable plastic bag. Refrigerate for at least 2 hours and up to 4 hours.

Prepare a grill. When the coals are glowing red, after 15 to 20 minutes, cover with the grate. After 5 minutes, use a wire brush to thoroughly clean the grate. When the coals are covered with a pale gray ash and you can leave your hand 5 inches above the fire for 2 to 3 seconds, the coals are ready.

To cook, remove as much marinade as possible from the shrimp. Thread the shrimp on skewers and sprinkle all sides with the remaining teaspoon of salt and the pepper. Place the kabobs on the grate and grill, turning once, until the shrimp are golden brown and firm, about 2 minutes per side. Transfer to a serving platter and serve immediately, garnished with the lemon.

Beef with Herb Butter ● ● ● ● ● ● ●

SERVES 6

I can vividly remember the first time I saw someone put butter on a steak: I was at Hilltop Steak House on Route 1 in Saugus, MA, widely known for its huge portions and extremely realistic fiberglass cows grazing out front. There were about 10 of us having dinner and one woman, who arrived late, asked for butter to put on her steak. I was both amazed and horrified. It took me years to overcome my aversion and when I finally did, I was so sorry for all I had missed. You don't need much butter to add a huge amount of flavor and there is something about the combination that is out of this world. Additionally, the butter dresses it up, making this kabob perfect for a dinner party: just add a Caesar salad and crusty bread.

This herb butter calls for all fresh herbs except tarragon because, in my experience, it's easy to use up the other herbs but tarragon tends to get tossed out. If you have fresh tarragon, by all means use it: substitute 1 tablespoon fresh for the 1 teaspoon dried. Don't be surprised if your guests slather on the butter—the recipe makes plenty and it's great to freeze. The butter is also great as a substitute for garlic butter on bread, pasta and shrimp and on roasted and baked potatoes.

FOR THE HERB BUTTER:

½ cup unsalted butter, at room temperature

1 tablespoon chopped fresh rosemary leaves

2 teaspoons fresh thyme leaves

2 garlic cloves, minced

1 teaspoon dried tarragon leaves

2 teaspoons kosher salt

1 teaspoon freshly ground black pepper

¼ cup finely chopped Italian flat leaf parsley leaves

3 pounds sirloin tips, left in long, thin strips, or top blade steaks, trimmed of fat and cut into 1¼-inch cubes

½ teaspoon freshly ground black pepper

To make the herb butter: Place the butter in a 1-quart bowl and, using a fork, mash until it is creamy and smooth. Add the rosemary, thyme, garlic, tarragon, 1 teaspoon of the salt, and ½ teaspoon of the pepper and mix until they are well incorporated into the butter. Place the mixture on a large piece of wax paper and form into a log. Roll into a column and transfer to a resealable plastic bag. Use immediately or cover and refrigerate for 2 weeks or freeze for up to 2 months.

Prepare a grill. When the coals are glowing red, after 15 to 20 minutes, cover with the grate. After 5 minutes, use a wire brush to thoroughly clean the grate. When the coals are covered with a pale gray ash and you can leave your hand 5 inches above the fire for 2 seconds, the coals are ready.

To cook, thread the beef on skewers and sprinkle all sides with the remaining teaspoon of salt and ½ teaspoon of the pepper. Place the kabobs on the grate and grill, turning every 1½ minutes, until the beef is deeply browned on the outside and rare in the inside, 8 to 10 minutes total. Transfer to a serving platter, coat with the butter and serve immediately.

Chicken Tandoori ● ● ● ● ● ● ● ● ●

SERVES 6

Tandoori refers to the tandoor, the traditional Indian clay oven in which food is cooked at a very high temperature. My version is a close relative of the authentic dish, although instead of including tomato sauce in the marinade, I add cherry tomatoes to the skewers. Try serving these with olive oil brushed pita bread.

¾ cup buttermilk or yogurt

2 tablespoons olive oil

1 tablespoon chopped fresh ginger

4 garlic cloves

1½ teaspoons turmeric

1½ teaspoons ground cumin

½ teaspoon coriander

¼ teaspoon ground cardamom

¼ teaspoon ground cinnamon

¾ teaspoon chili powder

Zest of 1 lime

1½ teaspoons kosher salt

3 pounds skinless, boneless chicken breasts
    or thighs, trimmed of fat and cut into
    1¼-inch chunks

½ teaspoon freshly ground black pepper

1 lime, cut in 6 wedges

To make the marinade: Place the buttermilk, olive oil, ginger, garlic, turmeric, cumin, coriander, cardamom, cinnamon, chili powder, lime zest and ½ teaspoon of the salt in a non-reactive 3- to 4-quart bowl and mix until all the ingredients are well combined. Add the chicken to the bowl and mix until it is completely immersed in the marinade. Alternatively, you can transfer the mixture to a large resealable plastic bag. Refrigerate for at least 4 hours and up to 8 hours.

Prepare a grill. When the coals are glowing red, after 15 to 20 minutes, cover with the grate. After 5 minutes, use a wire brush to thoroughly clean the grate. When the coals are covered with a pale gray ash and you can leave your hand 5 inches above the fire for 2 to 3 seconds, the coals are ready.

To cook, remove as much marinade as possible from the chicken. Thread the chicken on skewers and sprinkle all sides with the remaining 1 teaspoon of salt and the pepper. Place the kabobs on the grate and grill, turning every 1½ minutes, until the chicken is well browned on the outside and no longer pink in the inside, 8 to 10 minutes total. Transfer to a serving platter and serve immediately, garnished with lime wedges.

Lamb with Rosemary and Mint ● ● ● ●

SERVES 6

This is a classic lamb recipe that is perfect for kabobs. Serve with steamed fava beans and a cucumber salad with yogurt or grilled zucchini.

Unlike meats marinated in red wine vinegar or other acids, this one can marinate longer. The purpose of marinating food for an extended period of time is to allow new flavors to sink in and also to tenderize the meat. Generally meat is best marinated in some sort of acid because that will break down its muscle fibers, thus acting as a tenderizer. However, marinating in citrus juice or vinegar will actually "cook" the meat, as it does in seviche, because of the high acidity levels. Red wine, while acidic, will not "cook" the meat but will break down its muscle fibers. Additionally, it is naturally a complementary flavor to most meats.

½ cup olive oil

½ cup red wine

¼ cup fresh mint leaves

3 garlic cloves, minced

1 tablespoon chopped fresh rosemary leaves

1½ teaspoons kosher salt

3 pounds boned lamb leg meat, trimmed of fat
    and cut into 1½-inch cubes

½ teaspoon freshly ground black pepper

To make the marinade: Place the olive oil, red wine, mint, garlic, rosemary and ½ teaspoon of the salt in a non-reactive 3- to 4-quart bowl and mix until all the ingredients are well combined. Add the lamb to the bowl and mix until it is completely immersed in the marinade. Alternatively, you can transfer the mixture to a large resealable plastic bag. Refrigerate for at least 4 hours and up to 8 hours.

Prepare a grill. When the coals are glowing red, after 15 to 20 minutes, cover with the grate. After 5 minutes, use a wire brush to thoroughly clean the grate. When the coals are covered with a pale gray ash and you can leave your hand 5 inches above the fire for 2 to 3 seconds, the coals are ready.

To cook, remove as much marinade as possible from the lamb. Thread the lamb on skewers and sprinkle all sides with the remaining teaspoon of salt and the pepper. Place the kabobs on the grate and grill, turning every 1½ minutes, until the lamb is well browned on the outside and no longer pink in the inside, 8 to 10 minutes total. Transfer to a serving platter and serve immediately.

Marmalade Mustard Pork ● ● ● ● ● ●

SERVES 6

I never appreciated marmalade until I tried to make it from scratch. *Tried* is the operative word here: I wanted to decrease the massive amount of sugar and failed. The high sugar content makes it unseemly to me for eating but perfect as an ingredient for cooking. I think of it as heavily citrus-ed sugar. Serve these sweet, slightly biting kabobs with steamed mustard greens and creamy polenta.

As the name implies, chili powder is made from dried, crushed chile peppers along with a variety of other spices including onions, garlic, cumin, cloves, coriander, and oregano. It is usually quite spicy and therefore used sparingly. Nonetheless it remains one of the most common spices in American kitchens.

¼ cup orange marmalade

¼ cup Dijon mustard

2 tablespoons fresh orange juice

½ teaspoon chili powder or ¼ teaspoon cayenne

1½ teaspoons kosher salt

3 pounds pork butt, boneless center cut chops or pork shoulder, trimmed of fat and cut into 1¼-inch cubes

½ teaspoon freshly ground black pepper

To make the marinade: Place the marmalade, mustard, orange juice, chili powder, and ½ teaspoon of the salt in a non-reactive 3- to 4-quart bowl and mix until all the ingredients are well combined. Add the pork to the bowl and mix until it is completely immersed in the marinade. Alternatively, you can transfer the mixture to a large resealable plastic bag. Refrigerate for at least 4 hours and up to 8 hours.

Prepare a grill. When the coals are glowing red, after 15 to 20 minutes, cover with the grate. After 5 minutes, use a wire brush to thoroughly clean the grate. When the coals are covered with a pale gray ash and you can leave your hand 5 inches above the fire for 2 to 3 seconds, the coals are ready.

To cook, remove as much marinade as possible from the pork. Thread the pork on skewers and sprinkle all sides with the remaining teaspoon of salt and the pepper. Place the kabobs on the grate and grill, turning every 1½ minutes, until the pork is deeply browned on the outside and medium rare in the inside, 9 to 10 minutes total. Transfer to a serving platter and serve immediately.

Spicy Chicken with Cilantro and Ginger ●

SERVES 6

Serve these spicy kabobs on a bed of rice with a side of sliced avocados, halved cherry tomatoes and endive.

⅓ cup olive oil

Juice of 1 lemon

⅓ cup fresh cilantro leaves

3 garlic cloves

1 teaspoon ground cumin

1 teaspoon ground coriander

1 teaspoon ground ginger

½ teaspoon cayenne

1½ teaspoons kosher salt

3 pounds skinless, boneless chicken breasts
    or thighs, trimmed of fat and cut into
    1¼-inch chunks

½ teaspoon freshly ground black pepper

1 lemon, cut into 6 wedges

To make the marinade: Place the olive oil, lemon juice, cilantro, garlic, cumin, coriander, ginger, cayenne and ½ teaspoon of the salt in a non-reactive 3- to 4-quart bowl and mix until all the ingredients are well combined. Add the chicken to the bowl and mix until it is completely immersed in the marinade. Alternatively, you can transfer the mixture to a large resealable plastic bag. Refrigerate for at least 4 hours and up to 8 hours.

Prepare a grill. When the coals are glowing red, after 15 to 20 minutes, cover with the grate. After 5 minutes, use a wire brush to thoroughly clean the grate. When the coals are covered with a pale gray ash and you can leave your hand 5 inches above the fire for 2 to 3 seconds, the coals are ready.

To cook, remove as much marinade as possible from the chicken. Thread the chicken on skewers and sprinkle all sides with the remaining teaspoon of salt and the pepper. Place the kabobs on the grate and grill, turning every 1½ minutes, until the chicken is well browned on the outside and no longer pink in the inside, 8 to 10 minutes total. Transfer to a serving platter and serve immediately with lemon wedges.

Shrimp with Curried Butter ● ● ● ● ●

SERVES 6

These are so amazingly delicious it's a shame to even try to describe them: sweet, spicy, crunchy and rich, they are best served with a grilled pineapple and avocado salad on watercress (with walnut vinaigrette) and to drink, a beer.

The curried butter is also good on steamed rice, steak, chicken and bread.

FOR THE HERB BUTTER:

4 tablespoons unsalted butter, at room temperature

4 tablespoons chutney (any kind is fine)

1 teaspoon curry powder

36 large peeled deveined shrimp, about 1¼ pounds

Olive oil

1 teaspoon kosher salt

½ teaspoon freshly ground black pepper

½ cup sweetened coconut, well toasted (see Note)

To make the butter: Place the butter in a 1-quart bowl and, using a fork, mash until it is creamy and smooth. Add the chutney and curry powder, and mix until they are well incorporated into the butter. Place the mixture on a large piece of wax paper and form into a log. Use immediately or transfer to a resealable plastic bag and refrigerate for up to 2 weeks or freeze for up to 2 months.

Prepare a grill. When the coals are glowing red, after 15 to 20 minutes, cover with the grate. After 5 minutes, use a wire brush to thoroughly clean the grate. When the coals are covered with a pale gray ash and you can leave your hand 5 inches above the fire for 2 to 3 seconds, the coals are ready.

Brush the shrimp with olive oil. Thread the shrimp on skewers and sprinkle all sides with the salt and pepper. Place the kabobs on the grate and grill, turning once, until the shrimp are golden brown and firm, about 2 minutes per side. Transfer to a serving platter, brush generously with the butter and serve immediately, sprinkled with the toasted coconut.

NOTE • TO TOAST COCONUT: Preheat the oven to 300°F. Place the coconut in a single layer on a dry baking sheet. Transfer to the oven and bake until golden brown, 10 to 12 minutes. Set aside to cool and proceed with recipe.

Pomegranate Pork ● ● ● ● ● ● ● ●

Made from boiled pomegranate juice, pomegranate molasses is an uncommon but increasingly popular ingredient. It is a thick, dark red liquid that is slightly sweet and sour in flavor, much like the taste of fresh pomegranate. It is useful in marinades as a more sophisticated alternative to sugar. It is readily available in most Middle Eastern markets, where it is often called "unsweetened pomegranate syrup." Serve these kabobs with lightly toasted walnuts, orange pieces and crumbled goat cheese on top of romaine leaves, drizzled with walnut oil.

The third most expensive spice in the world (behind vanilla and saffron), cardamom is a tangy-sweet spice heavily used in Indian cuisine. It is the main ingredient in chai tea.

¼ cup pomegranate molasses

¼ cup olive oil

1 tablespoon Hungarian paprika

1½ teaspoons kosher salt

1 teaspoon ground cardamom

3 pounds pork butt, boneless center cut chops or pork shoulder, trimmed of fat and cut into 1¼-inch cubes

½ teaspoon freshly ground black pepper

To make the marinade: Place the molasses, olive oil, paprika, ½ teaspoon of the salt and the cardamom in a non-reactive 3- to 4-quart bowl and mix until all the ingredients are well combined. Add the pork to the bowl and mix until it is completely immersed in the marinade. Alternatively, you can transfer the mixture to a large resealable plastic bag. Refrigerate for at least 4 hours and up to 8 hours.

Prepare a grill. When the coals are glowing red, after 15 to 20 minutes, cover with the grate. After 5 minutes, use a wire brush to thoroughly clean the grate. When the coals are covered with a pale gray ash and you can leave your hand 5 inches above the fire for 2 to 3 seconds, the coals are ready.

To cook, remove as much marinade as possible from the pork. Thread the pork on skewers and sprinkle all sides with the remaining teaspoon of salt and the pepper. Place the kabobs on the grate and grill, turning every 1½ minutes, until the pork is deeply browned on the outside and medium rare in the inside, 9 to 10 minutes total. Transfer to a serving platter and serve immediately.

Pork with Bell Peppers and Vinegar ● ● ●

SERVES 6

A few years ago I worked at *Cook's Illustrated* magazine in Brookline Village, MA. One of my first assignments was to work on the classic Italian dish Pork Chops with Vinegar Peppers, a rustic dish of slightly caramelized, very vinegary peppers on top of pan-seared pork chops. This combination is nicely suited to grilling kabobs and luckily the vinegar permeates the peppers as well as the chops. Roast potatoes and/or crusty Italian bread are just the right complement.

¾ cup white wine vinegar

¼ cup olive oil

2 fresh rosemary sprigs, leaves chopped

3 anchovy filets, minced

5 garlic cloves, minced

3 bell peppers, any color, seeded and
   cut in large dice

3 pounds pork butt, boneless center cut chops
   or pork shoulder, trimmed of fat and cut into
   1¼-inch cubes

1 teaspoon kosher salt

½ teaspoon freshly ground black pepper

To make the marinade: Place the vinegar, olive oil, rosemary, anchovy and garlic in a non-reactive 3- to 4-quart bowl and mix until all the ingredients are well combined. Add the peppers and pork to the bowl and mix until they are completely immersed in the marinade. Alternatively, you can transfer the mixture to a large resealable plastic bag. Refrigerate for at least 4 hours and up to 8 hours.

Prepare a grill. When the coals are glowing red, after 15 to 20 minutes, cover with the grate. After 5 minutes, use a wire brush to thoroughly clean the grate. When the coals are covered with a pale gray ash and you can leave your hand 5 inches above the fire for 2 to 3 seconds, the coals are ready.

To cook, remove as much marinade as possible from the pork and peppers. Transfer the sauce to a small saucepan and bring to a boil. Set aside. Thread the pork and the peppers on skewers and sprinkle all sides with the salt and pepper. Place the kabobs on the grate and grill, turning every 1½ minutes, until the pork is deeply browned on the outside and medium rare in the inside, 9 to 10 minutes total. Transfer to a serving platter, drizzle with the reserved marinade and serve immediately.

Chicken with Herbes de Provence ● ● ●

SERVES 6

Originally from France, herbes de Provence is a common mix of either fresh or dried herbs: usually thyme, marjoram, basil, rosemary and lavender. While it can be purchased in most supermarkets, you can also assemble it on your own by tying the herbs together with a string. It is commonly used in stews or while grilling meat. Keep the theme by serving these kabobs with French potato salad with green beans and black olives, and French bread.

¼ cup olive oil

2 tablespoons herbes de Provence

Juice of 1 lemon

2 heaping tablespoons chopped Italian flat
   leaf parsley leaves

1½ teaspoons kosher salt

3 pounds skinless, boneless chicken breasts
   or thighs, trimmed of fat and cut into
   1¼-inch chunks

½ teaspoon freshly ground black pepper

To make the sauce: Place the olive oil, herbes de Provence, lemon juice, parsley and ½ teaspoon of the salt in a non-reactive 3- to 4-quart bowl and mix until all the ingredients are well combined. Set aside.

Prepare a grill. When the coals are glowing red, after 15 to 20 minutes, cover with the grate. After 5 minutes, use a wire brush to thoroughly clean the grate. When the coals are covered with a pale gray ash and you can leave your hand 5 inches above the fire for 2 to 3 seconds, the coals are ready.

To cook, thread the chicken on the skewers and sprinkle all sides with the remaining teaspoon of salt and the pepper. Place the kabobs on the grate and grill, turning every 1½ minutes, until the chicken is well browned on the outside and no longer pink in the inside, 8 to 10 minutes total. Transfer to a serving platter, pour the sauce on top, and serve immediately.

Scallops with Truffle Butter ● ● ● ● ●

SERVES 6

Very decadent but oh so simple. These kabobs are great as a first course with Champagne on New Year's Eve or Valentine's Day. If serving as a main course, accompany with sautéed leeks. Truffle oil can be found in most gourmet food stores and some better supermarkets.

FOR THE TRUFFLE BUTTER:

¼ cup unsalted butter, at room temperature

1 tablespoon truffle oil

2¼ teaspoons kosher salt

36 large scallops, about 3 pounds

Olive oil

½ teaspoon freshly ground black pepper

Place the butter in a 1-quart bowl and, using a fork, mash until it is creamy and smooth. Add the truffle oil and ¼ teaspoon of the salt and mix until they are well incorporated into the butter. Place the mixture on a large piece of wax paper and form into a log. Roll into a column and use immediately or transfer to a resealable plastic bag and refrigerate for up to 2 weeks or freeze for up to 2 months.

Prepare a grill. When the coals are glowing red, after 15 to 20 minutes, cover with the grate. After 5 minutes, use a wire brush to thoroughly clean the grate. When the coals are covered with a pale gray ash and you can leave your hand 5 inches above the fire for 2 to 3 seconds, the coals are ready.

Brush the scallops with olive oil. Thread the scallops on skewers and sprinkle all sides with the remaining 2 teaspoons of salt and the pepper. Place the kabobs on the grate and grill, turning once, until the scallops are golden brown and firm, about 2 minutes per side. Transfer to a serving platter, coat with the butter and serve immediately.

Chicken Thighs with Cumin and Coriander ● ● ● ● ● ● ● ● ● ● ● ●

SERVES 6

Cumin is a spice made from the dried and ground seeds of the cumin plant. It has a very distinctive pungent taste that some describe as "bitter-almond." Most often it is found in either curry or Middle Eastern and Mexican cuisines. Be careful not to confuse cumin with black cumin, which, although related, has a much stronger and spicier flavor. Serve these with lentils and steamed spinach.

½ cup olive oil

Juice and grated zest of 1 lemon

1 tablespoon minced fresh ginger

3 garlic cloves, minced

1½ teaspoons ground cumin

1½ teaspoons ground coriander

½ to 1 teaspoon cayenne

1½ teaspoons kosher salt

3 pounds skinless, boneless chicken breasts
   or thighs, trimmed of fat and cut into
   1¼-inch chunks

½ teaspoon freshly ground black pepper

1 lemon, cut into 6 wedges

To make the marinade: Place the olive oil, lemon juice and zest, ginger, garlic, cumin, coriander, cayenne and ½ teaspoon of the salt in a non-reactive 3- to 4-quart bowl and mix until all the ingredients are well combined. Add the chicken to the bowl and mix until it is completely immersed in the marinade. Alternatively, you can transfer the mixture to a large resealable plastic bag. Refrigerate for at least 4 hours and up to 8 hours.

Prepare a grill. When the coals are glowing red, after 15 to 20 minutes, cover with the grate. After 5 minutes, use a wire brush to thoroughly clean the grate. When the coals are covered with a pale gray ash and you can leave your hand 5 inches above the fire for 2 to 3 seconds, the coals are ready.

To cook, remove as much marinade as possible from the chicken. Thread the chicken on skewers and sprinkle all sides with the remaining teaspoon of salt and the pepper. Place the kabobs on the grate and grill, turning every 1½ minutes, until the chicken is well browned on the outside and no longer pink in the inside, 8 to 10 minutes total. Transfer to a serving platter and serve immediately with the lemon wedges.

Pork with Molasses and Fennel Seed ● ●

The combination of the sweet-tart molasses and the licorice-y fennel are among my favorites. I serve this on top of creamy polenta (add a little bit of heavy cream to a basic recipe) or alongside cornbread and a salad of watercress, apple and fresh fennel.

High in nutrients (especially manganese and calcium) and full of a deep rich flavor, blackstrap molasses is the byproduct of cane sugar processing, the syrup left over after the cane sugar has been boiled and the crystals have been removed. There are three grades of molasses, each one corresponding to the amount of crystals still remaining in the syrup. The third and final grade is known as blackstrap molasses because of its deep brown, almost black, color. It is used sparingly in most recipes because of its bitter flavor. Make sure that when purchasing, you buy "pure blackstrap molasses" rather than "blackstrap molasses diluted with corn syrup."

¾ cup balsamic vinegar

6 tablespoons blackstrap molasses

6 tablespoons olive oil

1 tablespoon Dijon mustard

3 garlic cloves, minced

1½ teaspoons crushed fennel seed

1½ teaspoons kosher salt

3 pounds boneless pork butt, boneless center cut chops or pork shoulder, trimmed of fat and cut into 1¼-inch cubes

½ teaspoon freshly ground black pepper

To make the marinade: Place the vinegar, molasses, olive oil, mustard, garlic, fennel and ½ teaspoon of the salt in a non-reactive 3- to 4-quart bowl and mix until all the ingredients are well combined. Add the pork to the bowl and mix until it is completely immersed in the marinade. Alternatively, you can transfer the mixture to a large resealable plastic bag. Refrigerate for at least 4 hours and up to 8 hours.

Prepare a grill. When the coals are glowing red, after 15 to 20 minutes, cover with the grate. After 5 minutes, use a wire brush to thoroughly clean the grate. When the coals are covered with a pale gray ash and you can leave your hand 5 inches above the fire for 2 to 3 seconds, the coals are ready.

To cook, remove as much marinade as possible from the pork. Place the marinade in a small saucepan and bring to a boil over high heat. Set aside. Thread the pork on skewers and sprinkle all sides with the remaining teaspoon of salt and the pepper. Place the kabobs on the grate and grill, turning every 1½ minutes, until the pork is deeply browned on the outside and medium rare in the inside, 9 to 10 minutes total. Transfer to a serving platter, drizzle with the reserved marinade and serve immediately.

Salmon with Garlic, Herbs and Pepper Flakes ● ● ● ● ● ● ● ● ● ●

SERVES 6

An easy and slightly spicy take on salmon that tastes as if you've spent hours in the kitchen, yet takes only minutes to prepare. Omit the red pepper flakes for a non-spicy version. Either way, serve with either polenta or steamed rice and grilled artichokes.

½ cup olive oil

2 tablespoons dry white wine

2 tablespoons fresh lemon juice

2 garlic cloves, minced

2 tablespoons fresh Italian flat leaf parsley leaves

2 tablespoons fresh mint leaves

¼ to ½ teaspoon crushed red pepper flakes

1½ teaspoons kosher salt

3 pounds salmon filet, cut into 2-inch strips

½ teaspoon freshly ground black pepper

1 lemon, cut into 6 wedges

To make the marinade: Place the olive oil, white wine, lemon juice, garlic, parsley, mint, red pepper flakes and ½ teaspoon of the salt in a non-reactive 3- to 4-quart bowl and mix until all the ingredients are well combined. Add the salmon to the bowl and mix until it is completely immersed in the marinade. Alternatively, you can transfer the mixture to a large resealable plastic bag. Refrigerate for at least 4 hours and up to 8 hours.

Prepare a grill. When the coals are glowing red, after 15 to 20 minutes, cover with the grate. After 5 minutes, use a wire brush to thoroughly clean the grate. When the coals are covered with a pale gray ash and you can leave your hand 5 inches above the fire for 2 to 3 seconds, the coals are ready.

To cook, remove as much marinade as possible from the salmon. Thread the salmon on skewers and sprinkle all sides with the remaining teaspoon of salt and the pepper. Place the kabobs on the grate and grill, turning every 1½ minutes, until the salmon is well browned on the outside but still rare in the inside, 7 to 8 minutes total. Transfer to a serving platter and serve immediately with the lemon wedges.

Spicy Buffalo Chicken ● ● ● ● ● ● ● ●

SERVES 6

The stories behind the origin of Buffalo chicken wings are very unromantic. Most of them go like this: a bunch of guys went into a friend's bar with growling stomachs. The guy's wife fried up some chicken wings, and instead of adding them to her chicken stock, and topped them with a spicy sauce. She grabbed some celery sticks from an antipasto platter, added some blue cheese dressing and the rest is history.

Best for an appetizer or on a buffet table, serve these kabobs with raw celery sticks.

3 tablespoons Dijon mustard

1 tablespoon plus 1 teaspoon Worcestershire
  sauce

1 tablespoon Tabasco sauce

1 tablespoon olive oil

Juice of 1 lemon

4 garlic cloves, minced

1½ teaspoons kosher salt

3 pounds skinless, boneless chicken breasts
  or thighs, trimmed of fat and cut into
  1¼-inch chunks

½ teaspoon freshly ground black pepper

FOR THE BLUE CHEESE DRESSING:

1 cup buttermilk or plain low-fat yogurt

1 teaspoon fresh lemon juice

¾ cup crumbled blue cheese

1 garlic clove, finely minced

½ teaspoon kosher salt

¼ teaspoon freshly ground black pepper

To make the marinade: Place the mustard, Worcestershire sauce, Tabasco sauce, olive oil, lemon juice, garlic and ½ teaspoon of the salt in a non-reactive 3- to 4-quart bowl and mix until all the ingredients are well combined. Add the chicken to the bowl and mix until it is completely immersed in the marinade. Alternatively, you can transfer the mixture to a large resealable plastic bag. Refrigerate for at least 4 hours and up to 8 hours.

While the chicken is marinating, make the Blue Cheese Dressing: Place the buttermilk or yogurt, lemon juice, blue cheese, garlic, salt and pepper in a 2-quart bowl and mash with a fork until creamy. Cover and refrigerate for at least 2 hours and up to 1 week.

Prepare a grill. When the coals are glowing red, after 15 to 20 minutes, cover with the grate. After 5 minutes, use a wire brush to thoroughly clean the grate. When the coals are covered with a pale gray ash and you can leave your hand 5 inches above the fire for 2 to 3 seconds, the coals are ready.

To cook, remove as much marinade as possible from the chicken. Thread the chicken on skewers and sprinkle all sides with the remaining teaspoon of salt and the pepper. Place the kabobs on the grate and grill, turning every 1½ minutes, until the chicken is well browned on the outside and no longer pink in the inside, 8 to 10 minutes total. Transfer to a serving platter and serve immediately with the Blue Cheese Dressing on the side.

Rosemary Garlic Beef ● ● ● ● ● ● ● ●

SERVES 6

These kabobs are perfect skewering on rosemary branches. Simply remove about ⅔ of the leaves (which you can use in the marinade), leaving about 1 inch of rosemary leaves on the top. Pierce the meat with the other end and thread until you get to the rosemary leaves.

Serve these skewered with lightly oiled zucchini and red onions and on the side, sugar snap peas or snow peas. If you don't skewer with red onions, serve with caramelized onions on the side.

2 tablespoons olive oil	1½ teaspoons kosher salt
1 tablespoon red wine vinegar	3 pounds sirloin tips, left in long, thin strips, or
2 rosemary branches, leaves chopped	top blade steaks, trimmed of fat and cut into
2 garlic cloves, minced	1¼-inch cubes
½ teaspoon crushed red pepper flakes	½ teaspoon freshly ground black pepper

To make the marinade: Place the olive oil, red wine vinegar, rosemary leaves, garlic, red pepper flakes and ½ teaspoon of the salt in a non-reactive 3- to 4-quart bowl and mix until all the ingredients are well combined. Add the beef to the bowl and mix until it is completely immersed in the marinade. Alternatively, you can transfer the mixture to a large resealable plastic bag. Refrigerate for at least 4 hours and up to overnight.

Prepare a grill. When the coals are glowing red, after 15 to 20 minutes, cover with the grate. After 5 minutes, use a wire brush to thoroughly clean the grate. When the coals are covered with a pale gray ash and you can leave your hand 5 inches above the fire for 2 seconds, the coals are ready.

To cook, remove as much marinade as possible from the beef. Thread the beef on skewers and sprinkle all sides with the remaining teaspoon of salt and the pepper. Place the kabobs on the grate, and grill, turning every 1½ minutes, until the beef is deeply browned on the outside and rare on the inside, 8 to 10 minutes total. Transfer to a serving platter and serve immediately.

Paul Sussman's Lamb Kabob ● ● ● ● ●

SERVES 6

Paul is a local chef and friend whose food I have been eating at each and every one of his restaurants, Daddy O's, Macondo and more recently, The Fireplace. Now I have the great honor and opportunity to work with him in a kitchen partnership at Z Square in Harvard Square and Marin County.

Serve these great kabobs with rice pilaf and grilled eggplant.

¾ cup olive oil

4 garlic cloves, coarsely chopped

3 tablespoons chopped fresh oregano leaves
   or 1 tablespoon dried

¼ teaspoon freshly ground black pepper

1 teaspoon kosher salt

3 pounds boned lamb leg meat, trimmed of
   fat and cut into 1½-inch cubes

3 Cubanelle peppers (also called frying peppers),
   cut into 1-inch squares

2 red onions, cut into 1-inch squares

FOR THE YOGURT SAUCE:

2 cups low fat yogurt

2 tablespoons olive oil

2 tablespoons fresh lemon juice

1 cup finely chopped English cucumber

¼ cup fresh mint leaves, finely chopped

2 garlic cloves, minced

To make the marinade: Place the olive oil, garlic, oregano, pepper and ½ teaspoon of the salt in a non-reactive 3- to 4-quart bowl and mix until all the ingredients are well combined. Add the lamb to the bowl and mix until it is completely immersed in the marinade. Alternatively, you can transfer the mixture to a large resealable plastic bag. Refrigerate for at least 4 hours and up to 24 hours.

While the lamb marinates, prepare the Yogurt Sauce: Place the yogurt, olive oil, lemon juice, cucumber, mint and garlic in a bowl and mix well. Cover and refrigerate for up to 3 days.

Prepare a grill. When the coals are glowing red, after 15 to 20 minutes, cover with the grate. After 5 minutes, use a wire brush to thoroughly clean the grate. When the coals are covered with a pale gray ash and you can leave your hand 5 inches above the fire for 2 seconds, the coals are ready.

To cook, remove as much marinade as possible from the lamb. Thread the lamb, peppers and onions on skewers and sprinkle all sides with the remaining ½ teaspoon of salt. Place the kabobs on the grate and grill, turning every 1½ minutes, until the lamb is well browned on the outside and still pink in the inside, 8 to 10 minutes total. Transfer to a serving platter and serve immediately with the Yogurt Sauce.

West Indian Chicken with Honey Butter ● ● ● ● ● ● ● ● ● ● ●

SERVES 6

Adapted from a recipe from *The Thrill of the Grill* by Chris Schlesinger and John Willoughby, I like to skewer these with slightly under-ripe bananas and serve with steamed rice and bitter greens.

The Honey Butter is also great on squash, carrots and sweet potatoes and, of course, bread.

FOR THE RUB:

1 tablespoon curry powder

1 tablespoon dried cumin

1 tablespoon paprika

2 teaspoons ground ginger

1 teaspoon cayenne

1 teaspoon kosher salt

1½ teaspoons freshly ground black pepper

3 pounds skinless, boneless chicken breasts
   or thighs, trimmed of fat and cut into
   1¼-inch chunks

2 slightly under-ripe bananas, cut into thick coins

Olive oil

FOR THE HONEY BUTTER:

¼ cup unsalted butter, at room temperature

¼ cup honey

To make the rub: Place the curry powder, cumin, paprika, ginger, cayenne, salt and pepper in a 3- to 4-quart bowl and mix until all the ingredients are well combined. Add the chicken to the bowl and mix until it is completely dusted with the rub. Alternatively, you can transfer the mixture to a large resealable plastic bag. Refrigerate for at least 2 hours and up to 24 hours.

While the chicken is marinating, make the Honey Butter: Place the butter in a 1-quart bowl and, using a fork, mash until it is creamy and smooth. Add the honey and mix until it is well incorporated into the butter. Place the mixture on a large piece of wax paper and form into a log. Roll into a column and use immediately or transfer to a resealable plastic bag and refrigerate for 2 weeks or freeze up to 2 months.

continued on next page

Prepare a grill. When the coals are glowing red, after 15 to 20 minutes, cover with the grate. After 5 minutes, use a wire brush to thoroughly clean the grate. When the coals are covered with a pale gray ash and you can leave your hand 5 inches above the fire for 2 to 3 seconds, the coals are ready.

To cook, thread the chicken and bananas on skewers, brush with olive oil and place the kabobs on the grate and grill, turning every 1½ minutes, until the chicken is well browned on the outside and no longer pink in the inside, 8 to 10 minutes total. Transfer to a serving platter, brush with the Honey Butter and serve immediately.

Kyle's Red Meat Rub　● ● ● ● ● ● ● ●

SERVES 6

Thirteen-year-old Kyle Rudman is my son Ben's friend and a budding chef. He especially likes to make rubs and this one is one of his favorites. When he gave a container of rub to me and Ben, we used it on steak that night and couldn't stop eating it until all the steak was gone. Then the next day, Ben put the rub on bread and couldn't stop eating that. Although Kyle says it's for red meat, it seems to be good on almost anything so consider doubling this recipe.

FOR THE RUB:

1 tablespoon kosher salt

1 teaspoon table salt

1 teaspoon freshly ground black pepper

2 teaspoons garlic powder

1 teaspoon onion powder

2 teaspoons Emeril's Original Essence
　spice seasoning

1 teaspoon KC Masterpiece® Seasoning

2 teaspoons minced dehydrated onions

3 pounds sirloin tips, left in long, thin strips,
　or top blade steaks, trimmed of fat and
　cut into 1¼-inch cubes

To make the rub: Place the kosher salt, table salt, black pepper, garlic powder, onion powder, Emeril's Original Essence, KC Masterpiece Seasoning and minced dehydrated onions in a 3- to 4-quart bowl and mix until all the ingredients are well combined. Add the beef to the bowl and mix until it is completely dusted with the rub. Alternatively, you can transfer the mixture to a large resealable plastic bag. Refrigerate for at least 4 hours and up to overnight.

Prepare a grill. When the coals are glowing red, after 15 to 20 minutes, cover with the grate. After 5 minutes, use a wire brush to thoroughly clean the grate. When the coals are covered with a pale gray ash and you can leave your hand 5 inches above the fire for 2 seconds, the coals are ready.

To cook, thread the beef on the skewers. Place the kabobs on the grate, and grill, turning every 1½ minutes, until the beef is deeply browned on the outside and rare in the inside, 8 to 10 minutes total. Transfer to a serving platter and serve immediately.

Spicy Pork with Orange and Chipotles ● ● ●

SERVES 6

Sweet and spicy, the flavors of this dish are nicely rounded out with a salad of bitter greens, like watercress, arugula and endive, served with chunks of creamy avocado. If you want more, mashed sweet potatoes are particularly perfect with the pork.

Made from dried, smoked jalapeños, chipotles are a brownish-red chile pepper either sold dried or in cans mixed with adobo sauce, a mixture of vinegar, garlic, soy sauce and spices. Chipotles themselves are spicy, so be sure to use with caution. They are most often used in marinades for meat, especially pork, in Mexican cuisine.

Add lightly oiled peaches and/or pineapple cubes to the skewer.

1 cup orange juice	1 ½ teaspoons kosher salt
2 tablespoons light brown sugar	3 pounds pork butt, boneless center cut chops
¼ cup safflower oil	or pork shoulder, trimmed of fat and cut into
3 tablespoons chipotles in adobo sauce	1 ¼-inch cubes
4 garlic cloves, minced	½ teaspoon freshly ground black pepper

To make the marinade: Place the orange juice, brown sugar, oil, chipotles, garlic and ½ teaspoon of the salt in a non-reactive 3- to 4-quart bowl and mix until all the ingredients are well combined. Add the pork to the bowl and mix until it is completely immersed in the marinade. Alternatively, you can transfer the mixture to a large resealable plastic bag. Refrigerate for at least 4 hours and up to 8 hours.

Prepare a grill. When the coals are glowing red, after 15 to 20 minutes, cover with the grate. After 5 minutes, use a wire brush to thoroughly clean the grate. When the coals are covered with a pale gray ash and you can leave your hand 5 inches above the fire for 2 to 3 seconds, the coals are ready.

To cook, remove as much marinade as possible from the pork. Thread the pork on skewers and sprinkle all sides with the remaining teaspoon of salt and the pepper. Place the kabobs on the grate and grill, turning every 1 ½ minutes, until the pork is deeply browned on the outside and medium rare in the inside, 9 to 10 minutes total. Transfer to a serving platter and serve immediately.

Horseradish Beef ● ● ● ● ● ● ● ● ● ● ●

SERVES 6

Until I did some research for this book, I had always thought a classic English ploughman's lunch was a roast beef sandwich with chutney, horseradish and cheddar cheese. It turns out that I was mistaken: a ploughman's lunch is more typically a cheese sandwich with chutney, a bottle of ale and an apple. As often happens with food, my mistake had a welcome outcome: this unusual kabob is one of my favorites and the taste does not expose its ingredients. For added authenticity, serve a romaine salad with cheddar and apples and for a further kick, raw fennel. Another great salad would be roasted beets, toasted walnut and frisée or mesclun. Roasted potatoes or garlic bread are also good additions.

"Civilization means food and literature all round. Beefsteaks and fiction magazines for all. First-class proteins for the body, fourth-class love-stories for the spirit." —Aldous Huxley

¼ cup chutney, any kind is fine

¼ cup bottled grated horseradish

¼ cup olive oil

2 tablespoons Dijon mustard

1½ teaspoons kosher salt

3 pounds sirloin tips, left in long, thin strips, or top blade steaks, trimmed of fat and cut into 1¼-inch cubes

½ teaspoon freshly ground black pepper

To make the paste: Place the chutney, horseradish, olive oil, mustard and ½ teaspoon of the salt in a non-reactive 3- to 4-quart bowl and mix until all the ingredients are well combined. Add the beef to the bowl and mix until it is completely covered with the paste. Alternatively, you can transfer the mixture to a large resealable plastic bag. Refrigerate for at least 4 hours and up to overnight.

Prepare a grill. When the coals are glowing red, after 15 to 20 minutes, cover with the grate. After 5 minutes, use a wire brush to thoroughly clean the grate. When the coals are covered with a pale gray ash and you can leave your hand 5 inches above the fire for 2 seconds, the coals are ready.

To cook, remove as much paste as possible from the beef. Thread the beef on skewers and sprinkle all sides with the remaining teaspoon of salt and the pepper. Place the kabobs on the grate and grill, turning every 1½ minutes, until the beef is deeply browned on the outside and rare in the inside, 8 to 10 minutes total. Transfer to a serving platter and serve immediately.

Greek Shrimp with Lemon and Feta ● ● ●

SERVES 6

Serve these Greek-inspired skewers wrapped in pita bread and on the side, hummus and tabbouleh, spiked with lots of fresh mint and fresh parsley leaves.

¼ cup olive oil

¼ cup fresh lemon juice

3 garlic cloves, minced

2 teaspoons dried Greek oregano

2 teaspoons chopped fresh rosemary leaves
  or ⅔ teaspoon dried

1½ teaspoons kosher salt

½ teaspoon crushed red pepper flakes

36 large peeled deveined shrimp,
  about 1¼ pounds

½ teaspoon freshly ground black pepper

⅓ to ½ cup crumbled feta cheese

1 lemon, cut into 6 wedges

To make the marinade: Place the olive oil, lemon juice, garlic, oregano, rosemary, ½ teaspoon of the salt and the red pepper flakes in a non-reactive 3- to 4-quart bowl and mix until all the ingredients are well combined. Add the shrimp to the bowl and mix until it is completely immersed in the marinade. Alternatively, you can transfer the mixture to a large resealable plastic bag. Refrigerate for at least 2 hours and up to 4 hours.

Prepare a grill. When the coals are glowing red, after 15 to 20 minutes, cover with the grate. After 5 minutes, use a wire brush to thoroughly clean the grate. When the coals are covered with a pale gray ash and you can leave your hand 5 inches above the fire for 2 to 3 seconds, the coals are ready.

To cook, remove as much marinade as possible from the shrimp. Thread the shrimp on skewers and sprinkle all sides with the remaining teaspoon of salt and the pepper. Place the kabobs on the grate and grill, turning once, until the shrimp are golden brown and firm, about 2 minutes per side. Transfer to a serving platter, sprinkle with feta cheese and serve immediately, garnished with the lemon wedges.

Orange Soy Chicken ● ● ● ● ● ● ● ● ●

SERVES 6

Before I started writing cookbooks, I worked at Legal Sea Foods in Newton, MA, with a woman named Quan. Quan used to make off-the-menu lunches for us, using combinations of ingredients I had never even considered, such as this one: soy and ketchup. Serve with steamed broccoli, broccoli rabe or spinach, and rice, of course. After all, that's what Quan did.

⅓ cup ketchup

⅓ cup frozen orange juice concentrate, thawed

2 tablespoons low sodium soy sauce

1 tablespoon Chinese chili-garlic sauce

3 pounds skinless, boneless chicken breasts
  or thighs, trimmed of fat and cut into
  1¼-inch chunks

Fresh cilantro leaves, chopped

Scallions, chopped

Chopped lightly toasted cashews (see Note
  on page 17 for toasting directions)

For the marinade: Place the ketchup, orange juice concentrate, soy sauce and chili-garlic sauce in a non-reactive 3- to 4-quart bowl and mix until all the ingredients are well combined. Add the chicken to the bowl and mix until it is completely immersed in the marinade. Alternatively, you can transfer the mixture to a large resealable plastic bag. Refrigerate for at least 4 hours and up to 8 hours.

Prepare a grill. When the coals are glowing red, after 15 to 20 minutes, cover with the grate. After 5 minutes, use a wire brush to thoroughly clean the grate. When the coals are covered with a pale gray ash and you can leave your hand 5 inches above the fire for 2 to 3 seconds, the coals are ready.

To cook, remove as much marinade as possible from the chicken. Thread the chicken on skewers, place the kabobs on the grate and grill, turning every 1½ minutes, until the chicken is well browned on the outside and no longer pink on the inside, 8 to 10 minutes total. Transfer to a serving platter and serve immediately, sprinkled with cilantro, scallions and cashews.

Scallops BLT ● ● ● ● ● ● ● ● ● ●

Perfect for a first course (just make half a recipe), lunch or light summer dinner.

A take-off on a classic BLT, serve these bacon-wrapped scallops with wedges of iceberg lettuce, halved cherry tomatoes and Green Goddess dressing.

18 bacon strips, about 1 pound, cut in half	FOR THE GREEN GODDESS DRESSING:
36 large scallops, about 3 pounds	2 tablespoons sour cream or full fat yogurt
½ cup fresh Italian flat leaf parsley leaves	2 tablespoons buttermilk
1 garlic clove, sliced	2 tablespoons mayonnaise
1 scallion, green and white parts included	1 tablespoon white vinegar
¾ teaspoon dried tarragon	1 teaspoon kosher salt
1 anchovy filet	½ teaspoon freshly ground black pepper
	Olive oil, for brushing

Wrap a bacon strip around each scallop. Secure with a toothpick and set aside.

To make the dressing: Place the parsley, garlic, scallion, tarragon and anchovy in a blender or food processor and process until smooth. Add the sour cream and buttermilk and blend until smooth. Add the mayonnaise and vinegar and mix by hand to combine. Transfer to a glass container, cover and refrigerate the dressing for up to 1 week. If the dressing separates, simply shake well.

Prepare a grill. When the coals are glowing red, after 15 to 20 minutes, cover with the grate. After 5 minutes, use a wire brush to thoroughly clean the grate. When the coals are covered with a pale gray ash and you can leave your hand 5 inches above the fire for 2 to 3 seconds, the coals are ready.

Brush the scallops with olive oil. Thread the scallops on skewers and sprinkle all sides with the salt and pepper. Place the kabobs on the grate and grill, turning once, until the scallops are golden brown and firm and the bacon is well browned, about 2 minutes per side. Transfer to a serving platter and serve immediately, dolloped with Green Goddess dressing.

Chicken with Cilantro and Soy ● ● ● ●

SERVES 6

Cilantro is a controversial herb: you either love it or hate it. I love it. Even though the cilantro is the primary flavor in this kabob, it's a good one for people who are on the fence, if there is such a thing.

Skewer these with lightly oiled peaches, zucchini and red onions. Serve with steamed rice.

3 tablespoons low sodium soy sauce

3 tablespoons fresh lime juice

¼ cup chopped fresh cilantro leaves

3 garlic cloves, minced

1 tablespoon minced fresh ginger

¾ teaspoon chili powder

3 pounds skinless, boneless chicken breasts
  or thighs, trimmed of fat and cut into
  1¼-inch chunks

1 teaspoon kosher salt

½ teaspoon freshly ground black pepper

1 lime, cut into 6 wedges

To make the marinade: Place the soy sauce, lime juice, cilantro, garlic, ginger and chili powder in a non-reactive 3- to 4-quart bowl and mix until all the ingredients are well combined. Add the chicken to the bowl and mix until it is completely immersed in the marinade. Alternatively, you can transfer the mixture to a large resealable plastic bag. Refrigerate for at least 4 hours and up to 8 hours.

Prepare a grill. When the coals are glowing red, after 15 to 20 minutes, cover with the grate. After 5 minutes, use a wire brush to thoroughly clean the grate. When the coals are covered with a pale gray ash and you can leave your hand 5 inches above the fire for 2 to 3 seconds, the coals are ready.

To cook, remove as much marinade as possible from the chicken. Thread the chicken on skewers and sprinkle all sides with the salt and pepper. Place the kabobs on the grate and grill, turning every 1½ minutes, until the chicken is well browned on the outside and no longer pink in the inside, 8 to 10 minutes total. Transfer to a serving platter and serve immediately, garnished with lime wedges.

Sweet Curried Steak ● ● ● ● ● ● ●

SERVES 6

I have been making this marinade for what seems like forever. Pal Susan Orlean gave me the recipe for flank steak—though she probably doesn't even remember—at least 25 years ago. The combination of flavors is amazing—sweet, salty, sharp and rich. The marinade is also good on pork chops and on chicken wings and legs and equally good hot or cold. I like to serve it alongside a salad of ripe mangoes and beefsteak tomatoes.

My dear cooking ally, Nancy Olin, routinely makes enough so she can have it cold the next day on white toast with mayonnaise and coarse salt.

"Mustard's no good without roast beef." —Chico Marx

¼ cup dry sherry

¼ cup Dijon mustard

3 tablespoons low sodium soy sauce

3 tablespoons light brown sugar

1½ tablespoons curry powder

3 pounds sirloin tips, left in long, thin strips, or top blade steaks, trimmed of fat and cut into 1¼-inch cubes

1 teaspoon kosher salt

½ teaspoon freshly ground black pepper

To make the marinade: Place the sherry, mustard, soy sauce, brown sugar and curry powder in a non-reactive 3- to 4-quart bowl and mix until all the ingredients are well combined. Add the beef to the bowl and mix until it is completely immersed in the marinade. Alternatively, you can transfer the mixture to a large resealable plastic bag. Refrigerate for at least 4 hours and up to overnight.

Prepare a grill. When the coals are glowing red, after 15 to 20 minutes, cover with the grate. After 5 minutes, use a wire brush to thoroughly clean the grate. When the coals are covered with a pale gray ash and you can leave your hand 5 inches above the fire for 2 seconds, the coals are ready.

To cook, remove as much marinade as possible from the beef. Thread the beef on skewers and sprinkle all sides with the salt and pepper. Place the kabobs on the grate, and grill, turning every 1½ minutes, until the beef is deeply browned on the outside and rare in the inside, 8 to 10 minutes total. Transfer to a serving platter and serve immediately.

Chris Schlesinger's Spicy Dry Rubbed Pork ● ● ● ● ● ● ● ● ● ● ●

SERVES 6

I've been adapting recipes from cookbook authors Chris Schlesinger and John Willoughby for years—even before we were friends. This time it was inadvertent: I was looking for ideas for ribs (not for this book) and looked in Mark Bittman's book, *How to Cook Everything*. Apparently he too borrows from his buddies. I like to serve these kabobs with cornbread.

FOR THE RUB:

1 tablespoon plus 1 teaspoon kosher salt

1 tablespoon plus 1 teaspoon Hungarian paprika

2 teaspoons ground cumin

2 teaspoons freshly ground black pepper

2 teaspoons chili powder

3 pounds pork butt, boneless center cut chops
    or pork shoulder, trimmed of fat and cut
    into 1 ¼-inch cubes

To make the rub: Place the salt, paprika, cumin, pepper and chili powder in a non-reactive 3- to 4-quart bowl and mix until all the ingredients are well combined. Add the pork to the bowl and mix until it is completely covered with the rub. Alternatively, you can transfer the mixture to a large resealable plastic bag. Cook immediately or refrigerate up to 24 hours.

Prepare a grill. When the coals are glowing red, after 15 to 20 minutes, cover with the grate. After 5 minutes, use a wire brush to thoroughly clean the grate. When the coals are covered with a pale gray ash and you can leave your hand 5 inches above the fire for 2 to 3 seconds, the coals are ready.

To cook, thread the pork on the skewers, place the kabobs on the grate and grill, turning every 1½ minutes, until the pork is deeply browned on the outside and medium rare in the inside, 9 to 10 minutes total. Transfer to a serving platter and serve immediately.

Sticky Chicken ● ● ● ● ● ● ● ● ●

SERVES 6

Although I have made these literally zillions of times (my children beg for them) using chicken wings, boneless and bone-in thighs and boneless and bone-in breasts, even when I use the same cut of chicken, they always come out slightly different. I often divide the recipe in half and add the crushed red pepper flakes to the half my fourteen-year-old daughter, Lauren, won't even look at.

Add fresh pineapple, zucchini and red onions to the skewer. This makes a perfect summer dinner with the addition of fresh corn on the cob and coleslaw.

½ cup low sodium soy sauce

¼ cup frozen orange juice concentrate, thawed

¼ cup light or dark brown sugar

2 garlic cloves, minced

1 small piece fresh ginger, peeled and minced

1 to 2 teaspoons crushed red pepper flakes
   (optional)

3 pounds skinless, boneless chicken breasts
   or thighs, trimmed of fat and cut into
   1¼-inch chunks

1 teaspoon kosher salt

½ teaspoon freshly ground black pepper

To make the marinade: Place the soy sauce, orange juice concentrate, brown sugar, garlic, ginger and red pepper flakes, if using, in a non-reactive 3- to 4-quart bowl and mix until all the ingredients are well combined. Add the chicken to the bowl and mix until it is completely immersed in the marinade. Alternatively, you can transfer the mixture to a large resealable plastic bag. Refrigerate for at least 4 hours and up to 8 hours.

Prepare a grill. When the coals are glowing red, after 15 to 20 minutes, cover with the grate. After 5 minutes, use a wire brush to thoroughly clean the grate. When the coals are covered with a pale gray ash and you can leave your hand 5 inches above the fire for 2 to 3 seconds, the coals are ready.

To cook, remove as much marinade as possible from the chicken. Transfer to a small saucepan and bring to a boil. Set aside. Thread the chicken on skewers and sprinkle all sides with the salt and pepper. Place the kabobs on the grate and grill, turning every 1½ minutes, until the chicken is well browned on the outside and no longer pink in the inside, 8 to 10 minutes total. Transfer to a serving platter, drizzle with the reserved marinade and serve immediately.

Tuna with Olives and Cumin ● ● ● ● ●

SERVES 6

I always keep green and black olives in my refrigerator. First, they make a good, no-nonsense, easy cocktail nibble and second, they add immeasurable flavor to salads, salad dressings and marinades. Even with a steady supply, I also always have olive paste on hand, for when I am feeling too lazy to chop.

Serve these kabobs with white cannellini beans and steamed spinach or a green salad with thinly sliced radishes.

½ cup black and green olives, chopped, or 3 tablespoons olive paste

⅓ cup olive oil

Juice and grated zest of 1 lemon

2 garlic cloves, minced

½ teaspoon ground cumin

3 pounds ahi or yellowfin tuna, skin removed, meat cut into 1-inch cubes

1 teaspoon kosher salt

½ teaspoon freshly ground black pepper

1 lemon, cut into 6 wedges

To make the marinade: Place the olives or olive paste, olive oil, lemon juice and zest, garlic and cumin in a non-reactive 3- to 4-quart bowl and mix until all the ingredients are well combined. Add the tuna to the bowl and mix until it is completely immersed in the marinade. Alternatively, you can transfer the mixture to a large resealable plastic bag. Refrigerate for at least 2 hours and up to 4 hours.

Prepare a grill. When the coals are glowing red, after 15 to 20 minutes, cover with the grate. After 5 minutes, use a wire brush to thoroughly clean the grate. When the coals are covered with a pale gray ash and you can leave your hand 5 inches above the fire for 2 to 3 seconds, the coals are ready.

To cook, remove as much marinade as possible from the tuna. Thread the tuna on skewers and sprinkle all sides with the salt and pepper. Place the kabobs on the grate and grill, turning every 1½ minutes, until the tuna is well browned on the outside but still rare in the inside, 7 to 8 minutes total. Transfer to a serving platter and serve immediately with the lemon wedges.

Chicken with Herb and Balsamic Marinade ● ● ● ● ● ● ● ● ● ● ●

SERVES 6

This marinade is basically dressed-up salad dressing. It's a great and simple way to tenderize and flavor chicken breasts or thighs. Serve with couscous and chopped fresh tomatoes and cucumbers sprinkled with crumbled feta or goat cheese.

Add lightly oiled peaches, pears, red onions and/or bell peppers to the skewer.

⅓ cup olive oil

3 tablespoons balsamic vinegar

3 tablespoons chopped fresh basil leaves

1 tablespoon fresh rosemary leaves or
   1 teaspoon dried

3 garlic cloves, finely minced

1½ teaspoons kosher salt

3 pounds skinless, boneless chicken breasts
   or thighs, trimmed of fat and cut into
   1¼-inch chunks

½ teaspoon freshly ground black pepper

To make the marinade: Place the olive oil, vinegar, basil, rosemary, garlic and ½ teaspoon of the salt in a non-reactive 3- to 4-quart bowl and mix until all the ingredients are well combined. Add the chicken to the bowl and mix until it is completely immersed in the marinade. Alternatively, you can transfer the mixture to a large resealable plastic bag. Refrigerate for at least 4 hours and up to 8 hours.

Prepare a grill. When the coals are glowing red, after 15 to 20 minutes, cover with the grate. After 5 minutes, use a wire brush to thoroughly clean the grate. When the coals are covered with a pale gray ash and you can leave your hand 5 inches above the fire for 2 to 3 seconds, the coals are ready.

To cook, remove as much marinade as possible from the chicken. Thread the chicken on skewers and sprinkle all sides with the remaining teaspoon of salt and the pepper. Place the kabobs on the grate and grill, turning every 1½ minutes, until the chicken is well browned on the outside and no longer pink in the inside, 8 to 10 minutes total. Transfer to a serving platter and serve immediately.

Five Spice and Lime Beef ● ● ● ● ● ●

If your guests aren't familiar with five spice powder, it will be almost impossible for them to guess what's in this marinade. A sweet and spicy seasoning often used in Chinese cuisine, five spice powder is usually a mixture of star anise, fennel seeds, Szechuan peppercorns, cloves and cinnamon.

Serve with steamed rice and roasted zucchini or butternut squash.

⅓ cup low sodium soy sauce

Juice and grated zest of 2 limes

2 teaspoons five spice powder

1 tablespoon finely chopped fresh ginger

4 garlic cloves, finely minced

½ teaspoon freshly ground black pepper

3 pounds sirloin tips, left in long, thin strips, or top blade steaks, trimmed of fat and cut into 1¼-inch cubes

1 lime, cut into 6 wedges

To make the marinade: Place the soy sauce, lime juice and zest, five spice powder, ginger, garlic and pepper in a non-reactive 3- to 4-quart bowl and mix until all the ingredients are well combined. Add the beef to the bowl and mix until it is completely immersed in the marinade. Alternatively, you can transfer the mixture to a large resealable plastic bag. Refrigerate for at least 4 hours and up to 6 hours.

Prepare a grill. When the coals are glowing red, after 15 to 20 minutes, cover with the grate. After 5 minutes, use a wire brush to thoroughly clean the grate. When the coals are covered with a pale gray ash and you can leave your hand 5 inches above the fire for 2 seconds, the coals are ready.

To cook, remove as much marinade as possible from the beef. Thread the beef on skewers and sprinkle all sides with the pepper. Place the kabobs on the grate and grill, turning every 1½ minutes, until the beef is deeply browned on the outside and rare in the inside, 8 to 10 minutes total. Transfer to a serving platter and serve immediately with the lime wedges.

Steak with Garlic, Oregano and Cumin ● ● ● ● ● ● ● ● ● ● ● ● ●

SERVES 6

The flavors in this marinade are from all over the map, but the Mexican influence (oregano and cumin) is the most prevalent so I like to serve these kabobs in a tortilla with rice, black beans and salsa. Guacamole, chips and a margarita or beer round it out nicely.

These are great skewered with cherry tomatoes, zucchini and red onions and/or bell peppers.

2 tablespoons canola oil

2 tablespoons red wine vinegar

2 tablespoons Hungarian paprika

1 tablespoon dried Greek oregano

3 garlic cloves, minced

2 teaspoons Dijon mustard

2 teaspoons ground cumin

1½ teaspoons kosher salt

3 pounds sirloin tips, left in long, thin strips, or top blade steaks, trimmed of fat and cut into 1¼-inch cubes

½ teaspoon freshly ground black pepper

To make the marinade: Place the oil, vinegar, paprika, oregano, garlic, mustard, cumin and ½ teaspoon of the salt in a non-reactive 3- to 4-quart bowl and mix until all the ingredients are well combined. Add the beef to the bowl and mix until it is completely immersed in the marinade. Alternatively, you can transfer the mixture to a large resealable plastic bag. Refrigerate for at least 4 hours and up to overnight.

Prepare a grill. When the coals are glowing red, after 15 to 20 minutes, cover with the grate. After 5 minutes, use a wire brush to thoroughly clean the grate. When the coals are covered with a pale gray ash and you can leave your hand 5 inches above the fire for 2 seconds, the coals are ready.

To cook, remove as much marinade as possible from the beef. Thread the beef on skewers and sprinkle all sides with the remaining 1 teaspoon of salt and the pepper. Place the kabobs on the grate and grill, turning every 1½ minutes, until the beef is deeply browned on the outside and rare on the inside, 8 to 10 minutes total. Transfer to a serving platter and serve immediately.

Citrus Chicken with Honey and Oregano ● ● ● ● ● ● ● ● ● ● ● ● ●

SERVES 6

Citrus sweet and herb-y, serve these kabobs with grilled artichokes and skewer with red onions.

3 tablespoons orange juice

2 tablespoons olive oil

2 tablespoons fresh lemon juice

2 teaspoons honey

1 tablespoon fresh oregano leaves

1½ teaspoons kosher salt

3 pounds skinless, boneless chicken breasts or thighs, trimmed of fat and cut into 1¼-inch chunks

½ teaspoon freshly ground black pepper

1 lemon, cut into 6 wedges

To make the marinade: Place the orange juice, olive oil, lemon juice, honey, oregano and ½ teaspoon of the salt in a non-reactive 3- to 4-quart bowl and mix until all the ingredients are well combined. Add the chicken to the bowl and mix until it is completely immersed in the marinade. Alternatively, you can transfer the mixture to a large resealable plastic bag. Refrigerate for at least 2 hours and up to 4 hours.

Prepare a grill. When the coals are glowing red, after 15 to 20 minutes, cover with the grate. After 5 minutes, use a wire brush to thoroughly clean the grate. When the coals are covered with a pale gray ash and you can leave your hand 5 inches above the fire for 2 to 3 seconds, the coals are ready.

To cook, remove as much marinade as possible from the chicken. Thread the chicken on skewers and sprinkle all sides with the remaining teaspoon of salt and the pepper. Place the kabobs on the grate and grill, turning every 1½ minutes, until the chicken is well browned on the outside and no longer pink in the inside, 8 to 10 minutes total. Transfer to a serving platter and serve immediately with the lemon wedges.

Lamb with Cumin, Cinnamon and Coriander ● ● ● ● ● ● ● ● ● ● ● ●

SERVES 6

Skewer these aromatic kabobs with fresh or dried apricots and tomatoes and serve with steamed rice with slivered almonds and chickpeas.

FOR THE CUMIN RUB:

2 tablespoons ground cumin

1 tablespoon plus 1 teaspoon ground cinnamon

1 tablespoon plus 1 teaspoon ground ginger

2 teaspoons ground coriander

$\frac{1}{2}$ teaspoon kosher salt

$\frac{1}{2}$ teaspoon cayenne

3 pounds boned lamb leg meat, trimmed of fat and cut into 1 $\frac{1}{2}$-inch cubes

Olive oil

1 lemon, cut into 6 wedges

To make the rub: Place the cumin, cinnamon, ginger, coriander, salt and cayenne in a 3- to 4-quart bowl and mix until all the ingredients are well combined. Add the lamb to the bowl and mix until it is completely dusted with the rub. Alternatively, you can transfer the mixture to a large resealable plastic bag. Refrigerate for at least 2 hours and up to 24 hours.

Prepare a grill. When the coals are glowing red, after 15 to 20 minutes, cover with the grate. After 5 minutes, use a wire brush to thoroughly clean the grate. When the coals are covered with a pale gray ash and you can leave your hand 5 inches above the fire for 2 to 3 seconds, the coals are ready.

To cook, thread the lamb on skewers and lightly brush with olive oil. Place the kabobs on the grate and grill, turning every 1$\frac{1}{2}$ minutes, until the lamb is well browned on the outside and still pink in the inside, 8 to 10 minutes total. Transfer to a serving platter and serve immediately with the lemon wedges.

Scallops with Citrus and Fennel ● ● ● ●

Even though citrus and fennel are in the marinade, these scallops are great atop a salad of romaine lettuce with raw fennel, pancetta and a lemon dressing.

½ cup orange juice

2 teaspoons olive oil

2 garlic cloves, minced

1 tablespoon dried fennel seed, chopped

1 tablespoon freshly grated orange zest

1½ teaspoons kosher salt

36 large scallops, about 3 pounds

½ teaspoon freshly ground black pepper

Chives, coarsely chopped

1 orange, cut into 6 wedges

To make the marinade: Place the orange juice, olive oil, garlic, fennel seed, orange zest and ½ teaspoon of the salt in a non-reactive 3- to 4-quart bowl and mix until all the ingredients are well combined. Add the scallops to the bowl and mix until they are completely immersed in the marinade. Alternatively, you can transfer the mixture to a large resealable plastic bag. Refrigerate for at least 4 hours and up to 8 hours.

Prepare a grill. When the coals are glowing red, after 15 to 20 minutes, cover with the grate. After 5 minutes, use a wire brush to thoroughly clean the grate. When the coals are covered with a pale gray ash and you can leave your hand 5 inches above the fire for 2 to 3 seconds, the coals are ready.

To cook, remove as much marinade as possible from the scallops. Thread the scallops on skewers and sprinkle all sides with the remaining teaspoon of salt and the pepper. Place the kabobs on the grate and grill, turning once, until the scallops are golden brown and firm, about 2 minutes per side. Transfer to a serving platter, sprinkle with the chives and serve immediately with the orange wedges.

Chicken Marbella ● ● ● ● ● ● ● ● ●

When the classic cookbook *Silver Palate* was published in the 80's, I devoured the book, cooking every recipe that intrigued me. I loved their Chicken Marbella and adapted it as I saw fit. It seemed, after a while, that every time I made it I furthered adapted it, eventually forgetting what was in the original recipe. This adaptation of an adaptation of an adaptation is wonderful served with couscous or grilled asparagus.

½ cup olive oil

½ cup red wine vinegar

½ cup white wine

3 to 4 garlic cloves, minced

1 tablespoon dried Greek oregano

1 tablespoon light brown sugar

1 bay leaf

1¾ teaspoons kosher salt

3 pounds skinless, boneless chicken breasts
  or thighs, trimmed of fat and cut into
  1¼-inch chunks

12 prunes

12 dried apricots

12 pitted green olives

½ teaspoon freshly ground black pepper

To make the marinade: Place the olive oil, vinegar, wine, garlic, oregano, brown sugar, bay leaf and ¾ teaspoon of the salt in a non-reactive 3- to 4-quart bowl and mix until all the ingredients are well combined. Add the chicken to the bowl and mix until it is completely immersed in the marinade. Alternatively, you can transfer the mixture to a large resealable plastic bag. Refrigerate for at least 4 hours and up to 24 hours.

Prepare a grill. When the coals are glowing red, after 15 to 20 minutes, cover with the grate. After 5 minutes, use a wire brush to thoroughly clean the grate. When the coals are covered with a pale gray ash and you can leave your hand 5 inches above the fire for 2 to 3 seconds, the coals are ready.

continued on next page

To cook, remove as much marinade as possible from the chicken; transfer the sauce to a small saucepan and bring it to a boil for 2 to 3 minutes. Discard the bay leaf. Thread the chicken, dried fruit and olives on skewers and sprinkle all sides with the remaining teaspoon of salt and the pepper. Place the kabobs on the grate and grill, turning every 1½ minutes, until the chicken is well browned on the outside and no longer pink in the inside, 8 to 10 minutes total. Transfer to a serving platter, drizzle with the reserved marinade and serve immediately.

Steak with Thyme, Shallots and Goat Cheese ● ● ● ● ● ● ● ● ● ●

SERVES 6

A take-off on the classic French combination of thyme and shallots, I like to serve these on their skewers with grilled bread and sliced tomatoes or on top of a salad of greens and tomatoes.

Although shallots, onions and garlic are all members of the onion family, they have distinct differences. Of the three, shallots and onions are more closely related and in fact, a shallot is really a variety of an onion. Onions, one of the most popular vegetables used in American cooking, consist of multilayered bulbs. There are twelve different varieties, all of which fall into two main subgroups: spring (sweet) onions and storage onions. Spring onions, including shallots, are harvested before they have matured, making them smaller, sweeter and milder. Storage onions, which are bigger and drier, contain the traditional onion flavor that Americans know so well. Garlic, a relative of the onion family, consists of one single bulb. Never store fresh garlic in the refrigerator, where it will lose its flavor.

FOR THE MARINADE:

½ cup olive oil

½ cup red wine vinegar

3 shallots, finely chopped

3 garlic cloves, minced

2 tablespoons fresh thyme leaves or
  2 teaspoons dried thyme

1½ teaspoons kosher salt

3 pounds sirloin tips, left in long, thin strips,
  or top blade steaks, trimmed of fat and cut
  into 1¼-inch cubes

½ teaspoon freshly ground black pepper

6 tablespoons crumbled goat cheese

To make the marinade: Place the olive oil, vinegar, shallots, garlic, thyme and ½ teaspoon of the salt in a non-reactive 3- to 4-quart bowl and mix until all the ingredients are well combined. Add the beef to the bowl and mix until it is completely immersed in the marinade. Alternatively, you can transfer the mixture to a large resealable plastic bag. Refrigerate for at least 4 hours and up to 8 hours.

continued on next page

Prepare a grill. When the coals are glowing red, after 15 to 20 minutes, cover with the grate. After 5 minutes, use a wire brush to thoroughly clean the grate. When the coals are covered with a pale gray ash and you can leave your hand 5 inches above the fire for 2 seconds, the coals are ready.

To cook, remove as much marinade as possible from the beef. Thread the beef on skewers and sprinkle all sides with the remaining teaspoon of salt and the pepper. Place the kabobs on the grate and grill, turning every 1½ minutes, until the beef is deeply browned on the outside and rare on the inside, 8 to 10 minutes total. Transfer to a serving platter and serve immediately, garnished with the crumbled goat cheese.

Swordfish with Dijon Tarragon Mayonnaise ● ● ● ● ● ● ● ● ● ●

SERVES 6

I hate mayonnaise, so when my friend Sharon Smith grilled swordfish with mayonnaise instead of olive oil I was extremely skeptical. Ever since that fateful day—after eating the tenderest swordfish ever—whenever I grill swordfish, I always slather it with mayonnaise.

Serve with artichokes, sautéed mushrooms and sautéed or fresh spinach.

½ cup mayonnaise

2 heaping tablespoons Dijon mustard

1 tablespoon fresh tarragon leaves

1½ teaspoons kosher salt

½ teaspoon freshly ground black pepper

3 pounds swordfish steaks, skin removed, meat cut into 1-inch cubes

1 lemon, cut into 6 wedges

To make the marinade: Place the mayonnaise, Dijon mustard, tarragon, salt and pepper in a 3- to 4-quart bowl and mix until all the ingredients are well combined. Add the swordfish to the bowl and mix until it is completely immersed in the paste. Alternatively, you can transfer the mixture to a large resealable plastic bag. Refrigerate for at least 3 hours and up to 24 hours.

Prepare a grill. When the coals are glowing red, after 15 to 20 minutes, cover with the grate. After 5 minutes, use a wire brush to thoroughly clean the grate. When the coals are covered with a pale gray ash and you can leave your hand 5 inches above the fire for 2 to 3 seconds, the coals are ready.

To cook, remove as much paste as possible from the swordfish. Thread the swordfish on skewers, place the kabobs on the grate and grill, turning every 1½ minutes, until the swordfish is well browned on the outside but still rare in the inside, 7 to 8 minutes total. Transfer to a serving platter and serve immediately with the lemon wedges.

Beef with Basil and Red Onion ● ● ● ●

SERVES 6

Many recipes allow substituting dried herbs for fresh herbs, but this isn't one of them. Most widely known as the main ingredient in pesto, fresh basil is a bright green leaf with a strong, almost spicy taste. It is best used within 3 days of purchase, although it can last for up to a week if refrigerated in a plastic bag. Once the leaves have begun to brown, you should toss out the bunch. Dried basil, sold crushed in jars, is not nearly as flavorful but works well in soups, rubs and some marinades.

Skewer with button mushrooms, bell peppers and tomatoes. Lightly rub with olive oil and sprinkle with kosher salt and freshly ground black pepper.

¼ cup red wine

¼ cup olive oil

¼ cup finely chopped red onion

¼ cup chopped fresh basil leaves

2 garlic cloves, minced

1½ teaspoons kosher salt

3 pounds sirloin tips, left in long, thin strips, or top blade steaks, trimmed of fat and cut into 1¼-inch cubes

½ teaspoon freshly ground black pepper

To make the marinade: Place the wine, olive oil, onion, basil, garlic and ½ teaspoon of the salt in a non-reactive 3- to 4-quart bowl and mix until all the ingredients are well combined. Add the beef to the bowl and mix until it is completely immersed in the marinade. Alternatively, you can transfer the mixture to a large resealable plastic bag. Refrigerate for at least 4 hours and up to 24 hours.

Prepare a grill. When the coals are glowing red, after 15 to 20 minutes, cover with the grate. After 5 minutes, use a wire brush to thoroughly clean the grate. When the coals are covered with a pale gray ash and you can leave your hand 5 inches above the fire for 2 seconds, the coals are ready.

To cook, remove as much paste as possible from the beef. Thread the beef on skewers and sprinkle all sides with the remaining teaspoon of salt and the pepper. Place the kabobs on the grate and grill, turning every 1½ minutes, until the beef is deeply browned on the outside and rare in the inside, 8 to 10 minutes total. Transfer to a serving platter and serve immediately.

Greek Chicken Kabobs ● ● ● ● ● ● ● ● ●

A take-off on the classic Greek salad, substituting chicken for the lettuce, serve these with tomatoes, cucumbers and feta cheese and if you want, Yogurt Sauce (page 46). Rice pilaf is a nice addition.

¼ cup fresh lemon juice

⅓ cup extra virgin olive oil

3 garlic cloves, minced

1 tablespoon dried Greek oregano

2 tablespoons finely chopped fresh mint leaves

1 ½ teaspoons kosher salt

3 pounds skinless, boneless chicken breasts
    or thighs, trimmed of fat and cut into
    1 ¼-inch chunks

½ teaspoon freshly ground black pepper

One lemon, cut into 6 wedges

To make the marinade: Place the lemon juice, olive oil, garlic, oregano, mint and ½ teaspoon of the salt in a non-reactive 3- to 4-quart bowl and mix until all the ingredients are well combined. Add the chicken to the bowl and mix until it is completely immersed in the marinade. Alternatively, you can transfer the mixture to a large resealable plastic bag. Refrigerate for at least 4 hours and up to 8 hours.

Prepare a grill. When the coals are glowing red, after 15 to 20 minutes, cover with the grate. After 5 minutes, use a wire brush to thoroughly clean the grate. When the coals are covered with a pale gray ash and you can leave your hand 5 inches above the fire for 2 to 3 seconds, the coals are ready.

To cook, remove as much marinade as possible from the chicken. Thread the chicken on skewers and sprinkle all sides with the remaining teaspoon of salt and the pepper. Place the kabobs on the grate and grill, turning every 1 ½ minutes, until the chicken is well browned on the outside and no longer pink in the inside, 8 to 10 minutes total. Transfer to a serving platter and serve immediately with the lemon wedges.

Scallops with Walnut Rosemary Butter ● ● ● ● ● ● ● ● ● ● ● ● ● ●

SERVES 6

Loosely adapted from *The Olives Table*, by Todd English and yours truly, these scallops are rich and buttery. Todd recommends serving them with raw fennel and shaved red onions; they're also great with a watercress salad with shaved Parmesan cheese. Either way, serve mashed potatoes.

FOR THE WALNUT ROSEMARY BUTTER:

3 tablespoons unsalted butter, at room temperature

3 tablespoons finely chopped toasted walnuts

¾ teaspoon finely chopped fresh rosemary leaves or ¼ teaspoon dried

1¼ teaspoons kosher salt

36 large scallops, about 3 pounds

Olive oil

½ teaspoon freshly ground black pepper

To make the butter: Place the butter in a 1-quart bowl and, using a fork, mash until it is creamy and smooth. Add the walnuts, rosemary and ¼ teaspoon of the salt and mix until they are well incorporated into the butter. Place the mixture on a large piece of wax paper and form into a log. Roll into a column and use immediately or transfer to a resealable plastic bag and refrigerate for up to 2 weeks or freeze for up to 2 months.

Prepare a grill. When the coals are glowing red, after 15 to 20 minutes, cover with the grate. After 5 minutes, use a wire brush to thoroughly clean the grate. When the coals are covered with a pale gray ash and you can leave your hand 5 inches above the fire for 2 to 3 seconds, the coals are ready.

Brush the scallops with olive oil. Thread the scallops on skewers and sprinkle all sides with the remaining teaspoon of salt and the pepper. Place the kabobs on the grate and grill, turning once, until the scallops are golden brown and firm, about 2 minutes per side. Transfer to a serving platter, coat with the butter and serve immediately.

Beef with Orange, Honey and Rosemary ●

I made this last New Year's Eve to great acclaim. Served with steamed spinach, grilled asparagus, roasted potatoes and a soft-leaf salad of Boston, red leaf and baby lettuces with crumbled goat cheese, it was the perfect meal to bring in the new year.

Juice and grated zest of 1 orange

¼ cup brown sugar or honey

¼ cup olive oil

3 garlic cloves, minced

2 teaspoons minced fresh rosemary

2 bay leaves

1½ teaspoons kosher salt

3 pounds sirloin tips, left in long, thin strips
　　or top blade steaks, trimmed of fat and cut
　　into 1¼-inch cubes

½ teaspoon freshly ground black pepper

To make the marinade: Place the orange juice and zest, honey, olive oil, garlic, rosemary, bay leaves and ½ teaspoon of the salt in a non-reactive 3- to 4-quart bowl and mix until all the ingredients are well combined. Add the beef to the bowl and mix until it is completely immersed in the marinade. Alternatively, you can transfer the mixture to a large resealable plastic bag. Refrigerate for at least 4 hours and up to 8 hours.

Prepare a grill. When the coals are glowing red, after 15 to 20 minutes, cover with the grate. After 5 minutes, use a wire brush to thoroughly clean the grate. When the coals are covered with a pale gray ash and you can leave your hand 5 inches above the fire for 2 seconds, the coals are ready.

To cook, remove as much marinade as possible from the beef. Thread the beef on skewers and sprinkle all sides with the remaining teaspoon of salt and the pepper. Place the kabobs on the grate and grill, turning every 1½ minutes, until the beef is deeply browned on the outside and rare on the inside, 8 to 10 minutes total. Transfer to a serving platter and serve immediately.

Portobello Mushrooms with Balsamic Vinaigrette and Shaved Parmesan Cheese

SERVES 6

These mushrooms can be skewered with many of the meat and chicken recipes but they were designed to eat as is. Serve them on a bed of greens, lightly dressed with additional dressing and garnished with shaved Parmesan cheese.

4 garlic cloves, chopped

2 teaspoons Dijon mustard

¾ cup balsamic vinegar

1 cup extra virgin olive oil

1 teaspoon kosher salt

½ teaspoon freshly ground black pepper

6 portobello mushrooms, cut into eighths

Shaved Parmesan cheese

To make the marinade: Place the garlic, mustard and vinegar in a blender or the bowl of a food processor fitted with a steel blade and process until thoroughly combined. While the machine is running, gradually add the olive oil. Add the salt and pepper. Place the mushrooms in a non-reactive 3- to 4-quart bowl, add 1 cup of the marinade and mix until the mushrooms are completely immersed in the marinade. Alternatively, you can transfer the mixture to a large resealable plastic bag. Refrigerate for at least 15 minutes and up to 1 hour. Reserve the remaining marinade for drizzling and for salad dressing.

Prepare a grill. When the coals are glowing red, after 15 to 20 minutes, cover with the grate. After 5 minutes, use a wire brush to thoroughly clean the grate. When the coals are covered with a pale gray ash and you can leave your hand 5 inches above the fire for 2 to 3 seconds, the coals are ready.

To cook, remove as much marinade as possible from the mushrooms. Thread the mushrooms on the skewers, place the kabobs on the grate and grill, turning once, until the mushrooms are deeply browned, about 3 minutes per side. Transfer to a serving platter and serve immediately drizzled with marinade and with shaved Parmesan cheese.

list of recipe titles by the week

KABOBS

RECIPES OF THE WEEK

Index